What Critics Say About
Travel Books
by Pamela Acheson Myers

"Insider tips and travel secrets."
— *Islands Magazine*

"A valid and nifty guide to wonderful places."
— *Naples Daily News*

"Pick this book up. It has a lot of great ideas."
— *News Center 6, Orlando*

"If you want to see the real British Virgin Islands,
this book is for you . . . offers a near-guarantee
of a great trip."
— *Independent Publisher*

"Essential to getting the most out of any trip
to the British Virgin Islands."
— *Midwest Book Review*

"Intimate knowledge of hotels, inns, bars,
restaurants, shops, and attractions."
— *Virgin Islands Weekly Journal*

Books by Pamela Acheson Myers

A Year in Palm Beach: Life in an Alternate Universe
The Best of St. Thomas and St. John, U.S. Virgin Islands
The Best of the British Virgin Islands
The Best Romantic Escapes in Florida, Volume One
The Best Romantic Escapes in Florida, Volume Two

PALM BEACH

A Complete Guide to the Island

**Sensational
Restaurants, Bars, Shops,
Beaches, Sports, Spas,
Events, Historical Sights,
Art Galleries, Happy Hours,
Museums, Maps,
Plus Seven Fabulous Walks
for Exploring the Island**

Pamela Acheson Myers

TWOMOOSE PRESS

Published by
TWOMOOSE PRESS
P.O. Box 2732
Palm Beach, Florida 33480
rbmten@gmail.com
386-690-2503

Credits
Author Photo: Damon Higgins, Palm Beach Post
Back Cover Photo, Town Hall: Pamela Acheson Myers
Back Cover Photo, Earl. E. T. Smith Park: Pamela Acheson Myers
Maps: Molly Aubry

Cover Design by Molly Aubry

Printed in the United States of America

ISBN: 978-1-892285-20-1

10 9 8 7 6 5 4 3 2 1

For
RBM

"It doesn't matter
how young or how old you are,
the time
to start using the good glasses
is right now."

— RBM

CONTENTS

SPECIAL FEATURES
AND
MAPS

ROYAL POINCIANA WAY

PALM
BEACH

ROYAL PALM WAY

ATLANTIC
OCEAN

LAKE
WORTH

WEST
PALM
BEACH

SOUTHERN BRIDGE

INTRODUCTION

Palm Beach: A Complete Guide to the Island *covers everything you might want to know to have fun in this town: the hidden vias along Worth Avenue, the many gardens and parks, the art galleries, where to find an ice cream cone or Dead Sexy jeans or an order of s'mores.*

This book tells where to dine under the stars, describes the best routes for scenic walks, and offers suggestions for finding everything from a perfect present to a delicious lobster salad.

Palm Beach is small. The year-round population is less than 10,000, although this number more than triples during the winter season. The entire town is on a barrier island that is 16 miles long and a little over half a mile at its widest point.

The Atlantic Ocean borders the east side, the Palm Beach inlet borders the north side, and Lake Worth borders the west side, separating Palm Beach from the mainland and from West Palm Beach.

Palm Beach and West Palm Beach are two entirely different places. Palm Beach is a town. West Palm

Beach is a city, with a population of over 100,000.

At the center of Palm Beach is legendary Worth Avenue. Here you will find numerous exclusive shops, chic restaurants, and high-end art galleries.

The location of Worth Avenue is unique. A lake and a grassy park are at one end and the Atlantic Ocean and a sandy beach are at the other end. You can be shopping in Salvatore Farragamo or Jimmy Choo or gazing at a painting by Helen Frankenthaler or Damien Hirst and then decide to stroll a block or two to the beach. Or you can walk a few blocks the other way and take a picnic to the lake. You don't need a car. It's all right here.

More stores and restaurants and art galleries are located about a mile and a half north of Worth Avenue, around Royal Poinciana Way.

Banks, a liquor store, a bookstore, and one or more drugstores can be found in the Worth Avenue area and in the Royal Poinciana area. The only supermarket on the island is one block north of Royal Poinciana Way.

1.
SHOPPING

Palm Beach's glamorous Worth Avenue, one of the world's legendary shopping venues, is lined with renowned (and expensive) shops — Ferragamo, Gucci, Tiffany, Max Mara, Jimmy Choo, Cartier, Chanel, and many more — plus petite versions of upscale department stores Neiman-Marcus and Saks Fifth Avenue. But tucked into courtyards, on side streets, and even on the avenue itself are wonderfully affordable and unusual shopping opportunities.

More Palm Beach shops can be found about a mile north of Worth Avenue, on and near Royal Poinciana Way. In this book, shopping is divided into two sections: the Worth Avenue area and the Royal Poinciana area.

Worth Avenue Area Shopping

Shops line Worth Avenue for three blocks, extending west from the Clock Tower at the beach to the corner of Cocoanut Row. It's a fascinating walk, whether you are a serious shopper or a resolute window gazer. To describe every shop on Worth Avenue would take a separate, full-length book. Below are descriptions of unusual or particularly interesting stores to explore that are on or within easy walking distance of Worth Avenue.

As you stroll along Worth Avenue, look for entrances to walkways, known locally as vias. Some are lined with small shops and others lead to stunning, peaceful courtyards with inviting shops, quiet seating areas, and the occasional restaurant. Don't miss these marvelous hidden spaces, if only to admire the appealing architecture and the many walls covered in brilliant bougainvillea.

DEPARTMENT STORES

The 100 block of Worth Avenue, the first block west of the beach, is where you will find the only two department stores on the island. On the south side, the commercial area is called the Esplanade (150 Worth) and several vias lead to a large two-story courtyard filled with shops and a Starbucks.

NEIMAN-MARCUS

This two-story showpiece of the legendary department store carries the best Neiman-Marcus has to offer, including designer dresses, lingerie, shoes, handbags, jewelry, and tableware. A compact but complete men's section is on the east half of the first floor. *151 Worth Ave., 561-805-6150.*

SAKS FIFTH AVENUE

This small, two-story jewel showcases the very best SFA has to offer. No, there isn't a floor just for shoes with its own zip code, as there is in New York City's Fifth Avenue store, but you will find a superb selection of designer day and evening dresses, plus pants, tops, shoes, and jeans. Next door (and connected) is a two-story men's store. *172 Worth Ave., 561-833-2551.*

BOOKS
CLASSIC BOOKSHOP
Stop here for best sellers, new releases, local-interest books, paperbacks, a large selection of enchanting children's books (Cheryl can lead you to the perfect choice), greeting cards, gift books, magazines, and newspapers, including *The Palm Beach Daily News* ("The Shiny Sheet") and the *New York Post. Mon.–Sat. 9am–6pm, Sun. 10a.m.–5p.m. Four blocks north of Worth Ave. 310 S. County Rd., 561-655-2485.*

CLOTHING (CHILDREN'S)
P.B. BOYS CLUB
Hot local shop for boys and men, featuring beachwear, swimwear, shoes, sandals, and beach towels, plus surfboard sales and rentals. *Four blocks north of Worth Ave., 307 S. County Rd., 561-832-9335.*

P.B. GIRLS CLUB
Popular spot to find girls' swimsuits, swim cover-ups, sandals, sneakers, T-shirts, sundresses, sweatshirts, and more. Also a section of the same for women. *Four blocks north of Worth, 309 S.County Road, 561-832-3596.*

CLOTHING (WOMEN'S)
55 CROISETTE
Stunning feminine leather jackets, shapely leather dresses and skirts in many colors, and handsome Balmain blazers, plus French and Italian shirts, shorts, and pants — pricey but well worth the cost. *Just north*

15

of Worth Ave., past Tiffany's. 415 Hibiscus Ave., 561-355-4244.

120% LINO
For perfect clothes for island living, head to this shop specializing in linen clothing in enticing colors (vibrant pinks, demure blues, can't-miss-me yellows) and pristine whites, fashioned into comfy dresses, classic shirts, knit T-shirts, casual tops, skirts, shorts, and pants. *333 Worth Ave., 561-833-0711.*

ALTONA
You can't beat Altona for a drop-dead, casual European look. Most clothes here are imported from France, and some are original designs by the French owner. Look for contemporary T-shirts, cotton and linen pants and unstructured jackets, and superb-fitting Dead Sexy jeans in many colors. *Courtyard inside the Esplanade, 150 Worth Ave., 561-832-0303.*

AMINA RUBINACCI
This sister store to Altona (*see above*) offers refined, casually elegant, mostly tailored, made-in-Italy clothing. Included are handsome, expensive (and expensive-looking) jackets, pants, blouses, sparkly sweaters, and sweater sets. *Courtyard inside the Esplanade, 150 Worth Ave., 561-832-0303.*

AQUA BEACHWEAR
Come here for bathing suits in a huge range of styles and colors. There are also cover-ups, beach dresses, and rash guards. *319 Worth Ave., 561-820-9555.*

BALATRO VINTAGE GALLERY
Outstanding collection of mint-condition, high-end designer vintage dresses, suits, blouses, and more, in-

cluding an especially large selection of Chanel, plus Gucci, Pucci, Versace, and Dior, among others. *Half block north of Worth Ave., past the Chanel store. 408 Hibiscus Ave., 561-832-1817.*

CALYPSO ST. BARTH

Follow the via to the petite courtyard and this enchanting shop featuring gauzy pastel-hued dresses, flowing pants, and beach cover-ups, plus casual sunwear, jewelry, sandals, pillows and rugs, candles, and fragrances. *End of the via at 247B Worth Ave., 561-832-5006.*

CASHMERE BEACH

Check out the entire floor-to-ceiling display of sensational French Sole flats and wedges. There are also three rooms of stylish, mostly casual pants, jeans, tops, skirts, sweaters, shirts, dresses, jackets, and handbags. *At the Peruvian Ave. end of Via Bice, 313 Worth Ave., 561-802-3300.*

C. ORRICO

A must stop for women and their teenage daughters, this shop features an extensive collection of Lilly Pulitzer and St. James as well as racks and racks of affordable dresses, pants, shirts, skirts, handbags, and jewelry. Some children's clothing also. *Three blocks north of Worth Ave., 336 S. County Rd., 561-659-1284.*

COURAGE B

Affordable jeans, leather handbags, colorful tops, and casual as well as dressy dresses. Also a large selection of lightweight, full-length sweater-y items perfect for chilly southern winter evenings. *325 Worth Ave., 561-429-6491.*

INTERMIX

Come here for totally trendy, fun, and occasionally wickedly outrageous silk shirts, shorts, jackets, jeans, and cocktail and nightclub dresses by Rag & Bone, Derek Lam, Alexis Guy, FRAME, Self-Portrait, Helmut Lang, and others. Wide range of prices, from very affordable on up. *218 Worth Ave., 561-832-4606.*

J.MCLAUGHLIN

On any given afternoon, probably half the women in Palm Beach are wearing smart tops or pants or dresses made from this shop's signature, magically non-wrinkling fabric, which is available in an ever-changing array of colorful designs. Also here are sweaters, handbags, belts, scarves, other accessories, and some clothes that are not wrinkle-proof. *225B Worth Ave., 561-655-5973.*

KAPSIKI

This one-of-a-kind Palm Beach gem is a showcase for beautifully crafted, mostly handmade blouses, sweaters, pants, jackets, jewelry, and handbags. Fabrics are exquisite and many items have a slightly '60s flower-child feel — long flowing skirts, blousy tops, and so forth. *235 Worth Ave., 561-832-7432.*

KATE SPADE

An array of quintessential Kate Spade dresses, shoes, jewelry, and purses, plus some of her ever-expanding collection of notepads, thank-you cards, champagne glasses, and other delights that we often discover we can't live without. *225 Worth Ave., 561-366-1384.*

MARLEY'S PALM BEACH COLLECTION

Come to this inviting shop for its charmingly displayed, affordable selection of colorful, comfortable tops and pants — prints and solids in linen, cotton, silk, and more. Also purses, hats, costume jewelry. *Via Amore Courtyard. 256 Worth Ave., 561-721-1022.*

PRETTY BALLERINA
A branch of the London boutique famous for ballet flats, this shop has walls and a display window featuring a dazzling selection of styles and colors. *Esplanade, 150 Worth Ave., 561-659-6670.*

RAPUNZEL'S CLOSET
Especially popular with the younger set, this trendy shop features casual, contemporary, not-too-pricey clothing. Lots of jeans plus comfy pants, tops galore (from T-shirts to silk blouses), sandals, jewelry, classy greeting cards, and nail polish in cool colors. Children's sizes are also available, plus a small selection of appealing children's books and toys. *326 S. County Rd., 561-659-5300.*

SANDOLO
Nothing will fit your feet better than sandals custom-made just for you by an Italian sandal-maker. Choose a style and get measured, and you'll soon walk away on air. Also, a selection of stylish ready-mades. *Via Amore Courtyard. 240 Worth Ave., 561-805-8674.*

CLOTHING (WOMEN'S AND MEN'S)
KASSATLY'S
The oldest boutique on the avenue, Kassatly's opened in 1933, is still owned and run by the same family, and has been patronized by generations of Palm Beachers. Don't be fooled by the window displays that are mostly lingerie: Yes, you will find beautiful nightgowns and robes here, but also fine linens (towels, sheets, tablecloths), Scottish cashmere sweaters, custom-made

shirts and jackets for men and women, and much, much more. *250 Worth Ave., 561-655-5655*.

ISLAND COMPANY
Don't forget that Palm Beach is an island, and nothing says "island-ready" quite like a shirt, a dress, or a bathing suit from Island Company. Come here for relaxed resort wear galore for men and women in summer white and colorful pastels and prints. Can't decide what to buy? Have a free rum drink at their on-premises bar while you think it over. *256 Worth Ave., 561-655-3231*.

MAUS & HOFFMAN
This longtime purveyor of traditional, fairly conservative menswear is a one-stop destination for many men, who drop in for everything from suits and sport coats to bathrobes, ties, shoes, and even umbrellas. Also, custom-made suits, shirts, and jackets. Small women's department. *312 Worth Ave., 561-655-1141*.

PETER MILLAR
If you haven't discovered Peter Millar menswear, now is the time. Casual, comfortable, and contemporary in a conservative sort of way, it comes in soft colors and fabrics, is well fitting, and is handsomely designed with attention to detail. Come here for pants, shorts, golf shirts, swim trunks, sweaters, a small selection of shoes, and accessories. Appealing women's clothing available in larger stores and online. *313 Worth Ave., 561-833-8332*.

STUBBS AND WOOTEN
A longtime hallmark of Palm Beach style, Stubbs and Wooten's ultra-comfy slipper shoes for men, women, and children are recognizable half a block away. Look

for a loafer-style shoe with an image — a tennis player, champagne glasses, or even the devil — across the forefoot. Customize a pair with your monogram, your varsity letter, or your own design. Be sure to stop in for their once-a-year summer sale. *340 Worth Ave., 561-655-6857.*

VINEYARD VINES

It all began with those highly recognizable men's ties with colorful, repeated patterns of tiny, often whimsical illustrations of almost anything: sailboats, road signs, pelicans, bull dogs, skiers, martinis. Now whole families come here to shop for a wide range of casual, totally preppy clothing, frequently imprinted with VV's iconic logo of a whale with a slightly idiotic grin. *305 Worth Ave., 561-659-5900.*

DOGS
BIBI'S DOGGY BOUTIQUE

Bibi offers "custom canine couture" — collars and leashes in a rainbow of colors and in a variety of leathers and canvas prints — plus comfy doggy beds in an array of appealing fabrics. Books for sale tell tales of Bibi, an adventurous Yorkshire terrier. *Via Amore Courtyard. 250 Worth Ave., 561-833-1973.*

GIFTS, HOUSEWARES, FURNITURE
BLUE PROVENCE

Palm Beachers rely on this shop for all things French, from caviar to foie gras to truffles, from porcelain dinnerware to tablecloths. A great many items are on display in this compact store, all sort of haphazardly arranged, so it pays to pause and take a good look around. Also, cakes and pastries baked daily and made to order. *Four blocks north of Worth Ave., 300 S. County Rd., 561-249-0522.*

IL PAPIRO

Produced in Florence, Italy, a wide selection of beautiful, handmade decorative papers, fine writing papers, leather journals, greeting cards, marbleized paper frames and boxes, custom invitations, note cards, and business cards. *347 Worth Ave., 561-833-5696.*

ISLAND HOME

White and pale blue predominate in this collection of captivating treasures for an island abode. Look for tropical, Caribbean-style tableware and table linens, lamps, candles, vases, chairs and end tables, and pillows galore. Also, a tiny selection of sundresses, tunics, and cover-ups. *334 Worth Ave., 561-832-6244.*

MARYANNA SUZANNA

The only way to truly appreciate the wealth of marvelous merchandise displayed here is to just stand still and look around very slowly. Tables and shelves are jam-packed with hand-painted Italian ceramic roosters, dishes, serving plates, pitchers, bowls, Murano glass, lamps, jewelry, and fancy soaps. Don't forget to look up and ogle the numerous chandeliers. Great place for gifts. *Halfway into Via Bice, 313 Worth Ave., 561-833-0204.*

MARY MAHONEY

Palm Beachers count on Mary Mahoney for upscale, tasteful "entertainment-ware," including fancy table linens, flatware, dinnerware, and decorative ice buckets and candleholders. Luxury brands include Baccarat, Lalique, and Christofle. It's safe to say something from Mary Mahoney graces almost every classy Palm Beach dinner party table. *336 Worth Ave., 561-655-8288.*

ROBERTA ROLLER RABBIT

This popular spacious shop features sheets, pillows, and duvet covers in colorful patterns and prints. Also, casual cotton beach bags, cover-ups, tops, and flowing dresses, plus packable jewelry for travel or the beach. *Esplanade, 150 Worth Ave., 561-833-4643.*

SHERRY FRANKEL'S MELANGERIE

A totally fun spot to shop and definitely the place to go when you desperately need a gift. The space is tiny but, floor to ceiling, chock full of wonderful and often whimsical surprises: colorful Limoges cocktail plates, painted wineglasses, fake wine spills, picture frames, plus numerous decorative pillows, guests towels, aprons, notepads, and bridge score pads imprinted or embroidered with cheeky, funny sayings. Many items can be personalized. *West end of Via Amore Courtyard. 256 Worth Ave., 561-655-1996.*

SILVER FUND

Don't be misled by the name. Come here for a divine selection of mint-condition vintage 1960s and 1970s furniture and accent pieces: sofas, chairs, tables of all kinds, ottomans, vases, picture frames, mirrors, lamps, and clocks — on and on it goes. All upholstered items have been gorgeously re-covered. And yes, there's also a major collection of Georg Jensen silver, hence the store's name. *330 Worth Ave., 561-629-5153.*

JEWELRY
BLUE CARIBE GEMS

Follow Via Parigi into the courtyard to find this inviting jewelry store with a welcoming staff and reasonably priced and striking necklaces, bracelets, bangles, rings, earrings, and more. Also, custom design plus jewelry and watch repair. *Via entrance just west of 347 Worth Ave., 4 Via Parigi, 561-833-1454.*

MYSTIQUE OF PALM BEACH
How about a dazzling diamond ring? Check out those glittery, shimmery bracelets, necklaces, rings, and earrings in the window display — all made with faux diamonds, rubies, sapphires, and emeralds! Prices, of course, are a fraction of what they would be for the real deal. *250 Worth Ave., 561-655-3008.*

SEQUIN OF WORTH AVENUE
Almost everyone walks out of here wearing at least one new bangle. Numerous baskets display irresistible and highly affordable bangles, bangles, and more bangles. Also bracelets, necklaces, earrings, charms, and more just right for the beach, travel, and casual wear. *219 Worth Ave., 561-328-8405; also 330 S. County Rd., 561-833-7300.*

TOYS
WHATCHAMACALLIT'S FOR KIDS
The child in everyone revels in this store's fabulous selection of toys, toys, toys aplenty! Puzzles, games, cuddly stuffed animals, wooden blocks, science kits, books, and kites for the beach. *Four blocks north of Worth Ave., 308 S. County Rd., 561-619-4806.*

WORLD-WIDE SHIPPING
Okay, admit it. You now have more shopping bags full of goodies than you have suitcases (and those were already full anyway). So how do you get all this stuff home? **RSVP** will ship anything anywhere. They will pick it up and pack it or crate it. And, if it's headed to NYC there's a good chance it will go north on their private truck. *277 Royal Poinciana Way, 561-659-9077.*

Royal Poinciana Way Area Shopping

Located about a mile and a half north of Worth Avenue, the north side of Royal Poinciana Way is lined with shops. The shopping area extends two blocks north to Sunrise Avenue and shops are also in the Royal Poinciana Plaza at the southwest end of Royal Poinciana Way.

BOOKS
PALM BEACH BOOK STORE

This full-service bookstore carries a complete selection of best sellers, numerous coffee table books, paperbacks, and children's books. Also, there's a Rizzoli section, and if you want to place a special order, just ask. *215 Royal Poinciana Way, 561-659-6700.*

CHILDREN
LIL RAPUNZEL'S

Need a special gift for a friend's new baby or even your own? This is the place to find darling baby clothes, delightful toddler toys, precious baby blankets, cuddly stuffed animals galore, and fashionable children's clothing. *251 Royal Poinciana Way, 561-659-3131.*

CHOCOLATE
PETERBROOKE CHOCOLATIER

Chocolate lovers have been known to feel faint when they amble into this "chocolatoreum" replete with irresistible treats: marshmallow and crunchy graham cracker s'mores, almond brittle, chocolate-covered popcorn, hand-dipped chocolate strawberries, and so much more! Those with a huge sweet tooth can feast on delightful, quite large replicas of animals, including winsome owls fashioned out of chocolate. *Outdoor tables. 253 Royal Poinciana Way, 561-557-8286.*

CLOTHING AND GIFTS
EVELYN & ARTHUR
The first of what are now nine stores located in resort areas across Florida, this large and popular boutique focuses on casual, mostly care-free, lightweight clothing for women: pants, tops, jackets, sweater sets, and scarves. *100 N. County Rd., 561-833-1551.*

GENTLEMAN'S CORNER
Even men who hate shopping often enjoy stepping into this cozy and inviting shop. Comfortable, casual clothing for men is displayed in an appealing, easy-to-browse setting. Come here for a wide selection of colorful swim trunks, comfortable shorts and pants, shirts, whimsical socks, handsome sweaters, Peter Millar items, leather belts, and more. *235 Royal Poinciana Way, 561-345-3660.*

MILDRED HOIT
A landmark Palm Beach shop that locals head to year after year for fashionable dressy and casual clothing for women, including silk blouses, fancy sweaters, casual tops, handbags, scarves, jewelry, pashminas, Crazy Larry pants, and jackets. Look for the two best-selling travel items: the elegant, easily packable, reversible "magic" coat every woman needs for wet and chilly weather (made of silk and fox and weighing less than a pound) and the never-iron Mary G. shirt, which comes in a rainbow of stunning colors. Check out the marvelous selection of winning gift items, many gorgeously pre-wrapped for one-minute shopping. The gift wrapping here is fabulously creative, so definitely have whatever you purchase gift wrapped, even if it's for yourself. *Ample parking in back. 265 Sunrise Ave., 561-833-6010.*

PALM PRODUCE RESORT WEAR
Among the jam-packed displays you'll find an ample collection of inexpensive women's casual, lightweight tops, pants, and bathing suits, plus purses, some shoes, and costume jewelry. There's also a small selection of men's shirts and shorts in the back. *217 Royal Poinciana Way, 561-835-9777.*

RSVP
A petite assortment of gifts, souvenirs, beach cover-ups and dresses, hats, and excellent greeting cards are in the front of this store, which actually specializes in shipping anything, anywhere in the world (*see page 24*). *277 Royal Poinciana Way, 561-659-9077.*

JEWELRY
ANGELO'S JEWELRY
Come here for a lovely array of necklaces, bracelets, earrings, and more, as well as a fine selection of estate jewelry. Knowledgeable owner. Custom design is also a specialty here, as is jewelry repair. *340 Royal Poinciana Way, 561-659-7303.*

VINTAGE LINENS
TROUSSEAU
Almost nothing is softer than a vintage napkin made of 100% linen. Shop here for fabulous, high-end vintage tablecloths, napkins, placemats, kitchen towels, bathroom guest towels, and more. Many are beautifully embroidered. A great spot to pick up perfect cocktail napkins. *In the middle of the Via. 219 Royal Poinciana Way, #1, 561-832-9696.*

27

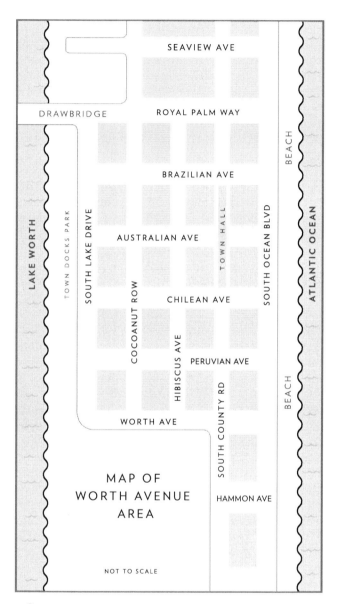

MAP OF
WORTH AVENUE
AREA

NOT TO SCALE

2.
THRIFT AND CONSIGNMENT SHOPS

If you have ever wanted to wrap yourself in a Brunello Cucinelli sweater or slip your foot into a $2,000 Manolo Blahnik stiletto lizard sandal, or sashay out to dinner in a classy Dior or Dolce & Gabbana or Armani but didn't want to pay the price, well . . . there's another way. In Palm Beach, thrift and consignment shops are show-cases for designer clothing. Some Palm Beach women wear a pricey designer item only once (or even not at all) and then donate or consign it. There are absolutely fabulous deals in this town. Many, many pieces of clothing that look absolutely new are available for a tenth, or even way less, of their original cost.

THRIFT SHOPS
CHURCH MOUSE
The queen of thrift shops, the Church Mouse is a treas-ure trove of pre-owned finds for just about everyone. Menswear includes suits, trousers, blazers, sport jack-

ets, and shoes. For women, look for designer suits, evening and cocktail dresses, jackets, silk blouses, handbags, lingerie, tops, shoes, and athletic wear. Also books, housewares, crystal, silver, and furniture. Closed June through September, but donations are welcome year-round and proceeds benefit Church of Bethesda-by-the-Sea outreach programs. *Two blocks north of Worth Ave. 378 S. County Rd., 561-659-2154.*

GOODWILL PALM BEACH BOUTIQUE
This small thrift shop carries a bit of everything, and some people head here especially for the monogram shirts (who cares if those aren't your initials.). *210 Sunset Ave., 561-832-8199.*

CONSIGNMENT SHOPS
"Consignment row" is one block north of Royal Poinciana Way, beginning on the corner of North County Road and Sunset Boulevard. Look for a row of shops on the south side of the street, starting on the corner with Classic Collections of Palm Beach and running west, including the vias, to Paradise Lost.

CLASSIC COLLECTIONS OF PALM BEACH
Come here for a wide and outstanding selection of truly top-of-the line women's clothing by famous designers (Armani, Helmut Lang, Dolce & Gabbana, Versace, Chanel, and many more), plus designer shoes, furs, and handbags. Also jewelry. *118 N. County Rd., 561-833-3633.*

PARADISE LOST
This shop is an excellent, upscale source for men's and women's designer clothing, shoes, and accessories, plus fine china, antiques, rare books, silver, and crystal. Its sister store, Paradise Boutique, one block north

30

at 227 Sunrise Boulevard, focuses just on women's fashions. *214 Sunset Blvd., 561-223-2284.*

FASHIONISTA
Located near Worth Avenue and not part of Consignment Row is this small but fully loaded collection of designer wear for women. Cocktail dresses, gowns, jackets, flashy designer bags — it's all here. *Four blocks north of Worth Ave., 298 S. County Rd., 561-249-6302.*

A PERFECT PALM BEACH DAY

A Starbucks cappuccino and a stroll along the beach.
A morning nap.
Shopping along Worth Avenue.
A late lunch outside at BrickTop's.
Another nap.
A cocktail at Café l'Europe while listening to David play the piano.
Perhaps another cocktail and dinner at Café Boulud.
An after-dinner drink and some make-your-own-s'mores at Chez L'Épicier.
Then a dance (or maybe ten) at the Chesterfield's Leopard Lounge.
And, finally, a walk to the beach to look for shooting stars.

SPLURGES AND EXTRAVAGANCES

Palm Beach. What better place to be extravagant and splurge a little, or maybe a lot? Isn't it time?

RENT A YACHT.
Feel like taking a spin around the ocean on an 111-foot luxury toy? *Call BiscayneLady, 305-379-5119.*

DRIVE A FANCY CAR.
Rent a Rolls Royce or a Lamborghini or a Ferrari for the day. *Call Prestige Luxury Rentals, 305-513-9711.*

SPRING FOR A SUITE.
The Chesterfield, the Colony, the Brazilian Court, and the Breakers have fabulous suites.

TRAVEL BY LIMO.
Leave the driving to someone else. Hire a driver, plan your day (or afternoon and evening) and sit back and relax. *Call Nino Zupljanin, 651-846-9225.*

GO FOR CAVIAR AND BUBBLES.
Most Palm Beach restaurants have superb and extensive wine lists. Order a special bottle of wine or champagne. Or what about caviar? Café l'Europe has a full caviar menu. During white truffle season, look for specials featuring this taste treat at many restaurants.

LUXURIATE IN A DAY AT THE SPA
Both Spa Cara and the spa at the Breakers resort offer a menu of half-day and full-day spa pleasures.

3.
RESTAURANTS

The island of Palm Beach offers a wealth of dining choices which range from the casual to the elegant and include Italian, French, and Asian options, among others. Restaurants are clustered in two areas, on and near Worth Avenue and on and near Royal Poinciana Way. To reflect this, the descriptions below are organized into two sections, Worth Avenue Area and Royal Poinciana Way Area.

Most Palm Beach restaurants are open 365 days a year and are exceptionally busy in-season and during holidays. Off-season (June or July through September), restaurants may close earlier in the evening, may be open fewer days, and may have reduced-price summer menus.

Dinner reservations are a good idea year-round, and essential from November through May. All the restaurants below, except for Cafe Via Flora, have a bar.

All Worth Avenue area restaurants described here have evening valet service, and most Royal Poinciana Way area restaurants also offer evening valet service.

WORTH AVENUE AREA
BICE
Gauzy white curtains and elegant striped chairs and sofas frame a long mirrored bar at this chic, contemporary spot. Decor is primarily white, accented here and there with brilliant gold. Classic Italian cuisine is served in two indoor dining rooms, one with a charming wall of French doors, and in a long, narrow outdoor dining courtyard. Excellent choices include Bice's signature chopped salad, minestrone, linguini with garlicky clams, butternut squash and ricotta ravioli, veal marsala, and tiramisu. Part of the Bice group, with restaurants in select locations worldwide, including Buenos Aires and Tokyo (the original Bice opened in Milan in 1926). *Two entrances. From Worth Ave. walk through Via Bice at 313 Worth Ave. or enter from 310 Peruvian Ave. Valet at 310 Peruvian Ave. Lunch, dinner daily 11:30a.m.–10:30p.m. 313 Worth Ave., 561-835-1600. $$$*

BRICKTOP'S
This restaurant is upscale, casual, and hugely favored by the in-season crowd, who flock here to join in the din and gobble up deviled eggs, grilled fresh fish, the BT signature meatloaf, the BT signature Palm Beach Salad (chopped shrimp, crab, avocado, tomatoes), excellent cheeseburgers, and steaks. Feeling decadent? Order the direct-from-the-oven, oversize chocolate chip cookie, topped with vanilla ice cream and hot chocolate sauce. It's large enough to share. Choose booths or tables in the wood-paneled dining room, booths in the bar, or tables on the outdoor terrace. Enormously popular with ladies (and gentlemen) who lunch, but it's also a wonderfully quiet retreat for a mid-afternoon late lunch. Reservations for lunch and dinner essential in-season. *Lunch, dinner daily*

34

11:30a.m.–10:00p.m. 375 S. County Rd., 561-855-2030. $$$

BUCCAN

One of a kind, this ultra-popular, contemporary, open-kitchen restaurant attracts a wide mix of clientele and is busy year-round. With a small plate/large plate menu that changes frequently, Chef Clay Conley manages to continually surprise and delight with original, imaginative, cross-cultural dishes and unexpected pairings of ingredients (short rib empanadas, squid ink orecchiette with Italian sausage and conch, snapper sliders with mango slaw). Also come here for one of the best burgers in town, dependably fresh oysters, and outstanding grilled fish. Reservations essential year-round. *Dinner Sun.–Thurs. 5–11p.m., Fri.–Sat. 5–12p.m. 350 S. County Rd., 561-833-3450. $$$*

CAFÉ BOULUD

The in place for locals and visitors alike, celebrity chef Daniel Boulud's upscale, elegant restaurant features unique, contemporary interpretations of French and other cuisines. Visit the romantic, multi-leveled, outdoor dining terraces, surrounded by tropical foliage, softly lit at night; the spacious, modern indoor dining room; the large, lit-from-within glowing bar; and the comfortable, sophisticated cocktail lounge. The changing menu might feature spanner crab fra diavolo, local swordfish with chanterelles and charred corn, hanger steak with bone marrow butter and pomme frites, and grilled bison loin with chimichurri. Ingredients and service are impeccable, and the artistically arranged plates even outshine the superb art on the walls. Chef Daniel is frequently on site, so don't be surprised if he comes by and asks how your dinner is. Impressive wine list and knowledgeable sommelier. Monthly wine-tasting dinners. Located in the Brazilian Court Hotel. *Breakfast daily 7a.m.–10:45a.m, brunch Sat.–Sun. 11:30a.m.–2:30p.m., lunch Mon.–Fri. noon–2:30p.m., dinner nightly 5:30p.m.–10p.m. 301 Australian Ave., 561-655-6060. $$$$*

CAFÉ L'EUROPE

Norbert and Lidia Goldner created this iconic Palm Beach restaurant in 1980 and moved it to its current location in 1995. To this day it remains one of the most elegant and glamorous restaurant settings on the island, with its floor-to-ceiling arched French doors, tray ceiling, numerous banquettes, brass accents, mirrored bar, table-top flower arrangements, fancy china, and live piano music. The cuisine is mostly European, and excellent choices include a traditional spaghetti bolognese, cappelacci Trasteverina (a pasta sheet wrapped around spinach and ricotta under a light tomato sauce), Wiener Schnitzel, and Long Island duckling. There's a caviar menu and, often, made-to-order dessert soufflés. Gracious service. Piano genius David Crohan showcases his broad repertoire nightly, except in the summer, when he heads north and other pianists take over. Sommelier Rainer Schonherr oversees the excellent wine list, and longtime general manager Bruce Strickland somehow remembers everyone's name and seating preference. Known for fabulous celebratory events: the Fourth of July, the Academy Awards, New Year's Eve, Halloween Costume Party. Unfortunately no longer open for lunch. Dinner *Tues.–Sun. (Wed.–Sun. off-season) 6:30p.m.–9:30p.m. 331 S. County Rd., 561-655-4020. $$$$*

CAFÉ FLORA

This is a charming setting for a casual, relaxing outdoor dining experience. Tables (many with large umbrellas to protect from rain or sun) are arranged in several courtyards, surrounded by colorful flower beds and walls covered with bougainvillea. Cuisine is primarily Italian and includes a selection of creative salads, burgers, pizzas, and sandwiches for lunch and, for dinner, pastas, veal, and chicken. Small indoor dinning room. *Lunch, dinner Mon.–Sat. 10a.m.–9p.m., Sun. 11a.m.–9p.m. 240 Worth Ave., 561-514-4959. $$*

CHARLIE'S CRAB

A good place to go if you want a view of the ocean while you have lunch. Tables are all inside, but many face the water. The menu includes salads, chowders, fish sandwiches and, for dinner, a large selection of cooked-your-way fish, plus steaks and chops. *Lunch, dinner Mon.–Thurs. 11:30a.m.–9p.m., Fri.–Sat. 11:30a.m.–10p.m., Sun. 11a.m.–9p.m. 456 S. Ocean Blvd., 561-659-1500. $$-$$$*

CHEZ L'ÉPICIER

The comfortable, almost plain, decor provides a perfect foil for the delightful cuisine served here. Sample the signature appetizer macarons (a creative twist on the classic French cookie) while perusing the original specialty drink menu and the wine list. The inventive, slightly playful menu defies categorization and offers something for everyone. Look for tuna tartare with sweet pea puree, grilled romaine with anchovies and Parmesan shavings, pan-seared foie gras with roasted shiitakes, zucchini "spaghetti" with basil and pine nuts, sweet pea risotto, braised short ribs with polenta, seared Chilean sea bass with cauliflower puree, a burger, and a giant grilled rib-eye. For what could be the most fun and whimsical dessert in Palm Beach, try the DIY S'mores (yes, you actually do grill your own marshmallows). Excellent service. *Dinner nightly 4:30p.m.–10p.m. 288 S. County Rd., 561-508-7030.* $$$

IMOTO AT BUCCAN
Chef Clay Conley plays with Japanese and other Asian flavors in this small, busy eatery next door to his well-loved Buccan. The ever-changing, ingenious menu might include an oyster-and-sake shooter, tuna and foie slider with mango salsa, and char sui pork belly bun with pickled cucumber. Come here for sashimi, wood-fired selections, nigiri, rolls, and so on. Like its big-sister restaurant, ingredients here are of impeccable quality. *Dinner Sun.–Thurs. 5:30p.m.–11:00p.m., Fri.–Sat. 5:30p.m.–12:00 midnight. 350 S. County Rd., 561-833-5522.* $$$

LEOPARD LOUNGE AND RESTAURANT
Mirrors and black lacquered walls provide a sophisticated backdrop for breakfast, lunch, and dinner at this popular spot in the Chesterfield Hotel. There is entertainment nightly and a small dance floor, and the bar attracts a large weekend crowd, so don't come here for a quiet dinner but rather to join in the fun. Lunch is a peaceful affair. Also, there's an outdoor courtyard for lunch and dinner. Be sure to check out the R-rated ceiling of dashing red swirls. Bea's homemade chicken noodle soup is a signature dish on the lunch and dinner menu. The cheeseburgers are a good choice as are the chopped salad, English fish and chips, and the Leopard Club sandwich. Steaks and chicken are on the dinner menu. *Breakfast 7a.m.–11a.m.; lunch 11a.m.–2:30p.m.; dinner Sun.–Thurs. 5:30p.m.–11p.m., Fri.–Sat. 5:30p.m.–midnight. 363 Cocoanut Rd., 561-659-5800.* $$-$$$

PIZZA AL FRESCO

Delightful, casual dining in a magical courtyard. Simple tables, many under umbrellas or palm trees, grace a tiled courtyard complex designed by the legendary architect Addison Mizner. What was once his private home is on the south side of the courtyard. Stucco walls are draped with dazzling bougainvillea. At night, palm trees sparkle with tiny twinkling lights. There are more than 20 outstanding ultrathin, crusted pizza offerings, plus fried calamari, baked pasta dishes, roasted chicken, roasted salmon, and the signature lobster salad. Also a charming indoor dining room and a bar. Reservations not accepted for lunch. Valet at 337 Worth Avenue, entrance in center of Via Mizner. *Lunch, dinner daily. 11a.m.–10p.m. 14 Via Mizner, 561-832-0032. $$*

POLO AT THE COLONY

This indoor/outdoor restaurant is located at the iconic Colony Hotel, which opened in 1947. In-season, ladies who lunch flock here to the outside tables facing the pool and dine on various salads (including a popular chicken curry salad), cucumber and egg salad tea sandwiches, and burgers. Also tables inside, as well as a popular bar. The dinner menu includes various steaks, prime rib, some fish and chicken offerings. *Open daily. Breakfast 7a.m.–11a.m., lunch 11a.m.– 3p.m., dinner 5:30p.m.–10p.m. 155 Hammon Ave., 561-655-5430 $$–$$$*

RENATO'S

This is a fabulously romantic restaurant. Dine in one of the three elegant indoor rooms, elaborately decorated in red and gold, or choose the stunning outdoor courtyard, with walls covered in brilliant bougainvillea blossoms and the sky above. Come here for superb

39

Italian cuisine including veal scaloppine, tagliolini alla Bolognese, risotto ai fungi, and osso buco. Be sure to check the daily specials, which include outstanding fish. Warm black olive dinner rolls are a treat. The wine list includes many fine choices. Valet at 337 Worth Avenue, entrance in center of Via Mizner. *Lunch Mon.–Sat 11:30a.m.–3p.m.; dinner nightly 6p.m.–10p.m. 87 Via Mizner, 561-655-9752. $$$*

TABOO
A landmark in Palm Beach since 1945, Taboo continues to be the go-to spot for a varied menu, great people watching, and casual comfort. There's a small front dining area with a coveted front window table, as well as a long bar and three additional dining areas in back, one with a gas-burning fireplace. The varied menu has something for everyone: burgers, steaks, salads, seafood, chili, and small plates. A fabulous bar, with two small soundless built-in TVs tucked up high at each end, a large fish tank in the middle, and Bobby, absolutely the best bartender in Palm Beach. Note to the ladies: When you head to the head, that right-hand door leads to a third bathroom. *Daily 11:30a.m.–10:00p.m. (last order taken at 9:59p.m.). Menu switches from lunch to dinner at 5p.m. Also walk-in entrance from Peruvian, across from Club Colette. 221 Worth Avenue, 561-835-3500. $$*

ROYAL POINCIANA WAY AREA
CHEZ JEAN-PIERRE BISTRO
This quintessentially classic French restaurant is wildly popular with Palm Beachers. They come here for scrambled eggs with caviar (served in the shell), tasty tomato tartare salad, always-in-demand Dover sole, roasted duck, outstanding pomme frites, and delicious chocolate profiteroles. Banquettes face the bar

and many tables are in a peak-ceilinged dining room hung with an eclectic selection of art. Congenial bar. Excellent wine list. *Valet and walk-in entrance just west of N. County Rd. on Sunset Ave (first driveway on north side). Dinner Mon.–Sat. 5:30p.m.– 10:30p.m. 132 N. County Rd., 561-833-1171. $$$$*

CUCINA DELL' ARTE
The small outdoor terrace facing Royal Poinciana Way is busy for breakfast, lunch, and dinner. Indoors are two small dining areas and a U-shaped bar. The extensive breakfast menu includes avocado toast, omelets, French toast, and eggs any way. Lunch and dinner offerings are primarily Italian — bruschetta, pizzas, eggplant parmigiano, linguini with clams. Bar stays open until 3:00 a.m. and bartenders head here after work for late night fun. *Breakfast, lunch, dinner, snacks 7a.m.–midnight (bar open until 3a.m.). 257 Royal Poinciana Way, 561-655-0770. $$*

ECHO
Red and black decor provide the setting for an evening of Chinese, Japanese, Thai, Vietnamese, and Korean cuisine. The extensive Asian menu includes a selection of sushi and sashimi, a large variety of traditional and specialty rolls, dim sum, stir-fry dishes, noodles, and more. *Dinner Tues.–Sun. 5p.m.–10p.m. 230 Sunrise Ave., 561-655-6611. $$$*

FLAGLER STEAKHOUSE AT THE BREAKERS
Located across South County Road from the Breakers, this classic steak house offers a wide range of steaks, plus fish, chicken, and pasta dishes and a large selection of sides, including creamed spinach. Dine inside or on the terrace overlooking the golf course. Lighter fare including Cobb salad, omelets, and sandwiches

are on the lunch menu. *Lunch 11:30a.m.–3p.m., dinner 5:30p.m.–9p.m., Sun. brunch 11a.m.–3p.m. 2 S. County Rd., 561-655-6611. $$$–$$$$*

MEAT MARKET
Contemporary, slightly glitzy decor is the setting for this always packed and expensive beef lover's paradise. A mouthwatering menu of top-quality steaks and fancy steak butters (lobster, marrow, Boursin) and sauces (horseradish truffle, mango and Scotch bonnet, signature A-100) are the draw here. Also hearty sides (mac and cheese, lobster mashed potatoes, creamed spinach, gouda tater tots). A few steaks are available in half sizes, but portions are generally ample, and although there are seafood and fish selections on the menu, this is not the place to come when you want a light meal. *Dinner Sun.–Thurs. 4p.m.–10p.m., Fri.–Sat. 4p.m.–11p.m. 191 Bradley Place, 561-354-9800. $$$$*

NICK AND JOHNNIE'S
Except on really hot summer days, the outdoor terrace facing Royal Poinciana is a fine spot for lunch, dinner, or Sunday brunch. This casual restaurant features many salads plus burgers, sandwiches, tacos, and steaks. *Sun.–Thurs. 11a.m.–9p.m., Fri.–Sat. 11a.m.–10p.m., Sun. 10a.m.–9p.m. 207 Royal Poinciana Way, 561-655-3319. $$*

PALM BEACH GRILL
One of the town's most sought-after dining destinations year-round, the Palm Beach Grill is a totally happening place. It's owned by the Hillstone Restaurant Group (Houston's, Rutherford Grill, R+D Kitchen, among others), whose eateries are revered — even by restaurant critics — for impeccable ingredients, re-

markable consistency, and outstanding service. The noisy but appealing atmosphere invites one to join in the fun and be part of the crowd. Tables and booths are in a dimly-lit contemporary dining room, and several high-top tables are in the bar area, which adjoins an open kitchen. The menu is across the board and you can't go wrong here: smoked salmon filet, heirloom tomato salad, a cheeseburger, crab cakes, fresh fish of the day, slow-roasted pork ribs, or the hot dog with everything. Desserts include a hot fudge sundae and key lime pie and sometimes (you have to ask) cookies. *Dinner Sun.–Thurs. 5p.m.–10p.m., Fri.–Sat. 5p.m.–11p.m. 340 Royal Poinciana Plaza, 561-835-1077. $$-$$$*

PB CATCH SEAFOOD AND RAW BAR

Regulars head here for the top-notch selection of outstandingly fresh fish and seafood. Choose from the innovative seafood charcuterie board (salmon pastrami, smoked mussel piperade, scallop mortadella), one of the many simple but creative fish and seafood dishes, or, when available, a two-and-a-half-pound Maine lobster. For purists, all fish can be simply grilled or sautéed. A few items, like baby back ribs and chicken paillard, are available for the nonseafood crowd. Oyster lovers often dine at the long, comfortable oyster bar, where the evening's selections of fresh oysters are displayed, nestled in shaved ice. The decor is contemporary, with clean lines and lots of mirrors. *Dinner Sun.–Thurs. 5:30p.m.-9p.m., Fri.-Sat. 5:30p.m.-10p.m. 251 Sunrise Ave., 561-655-5558. $$$*

SANT AMBROEUS

This chic Italian restaurant is all the rage from early morning until well into the night. Start your day here with a frothy cappuccino, return around lunchtime for a tasty panini, then head here at cocktail hour for fancy bar drinks before enjoying a filet mignon sprinkled with white truffles. Dine in the formal dining room or at the casual high and low tables facing the bar. Décor is typical Sant Ambroeus, including the signature wallpaper. There's a takeout counter, a showcase of Italian delicacies, plus gourmet items and gift baskets. Also in Southampton and New York City. *Sun.–Mon. 8a.m.–10p.m., Tues.–Sat. 8a.m.–11p.m., 300 Royal Poinciana Plaza, 561-285-7990. $$$$*

TESTA'S

Owned by the same family since 1921, this ultra-casual restaurant serves breakfast and sandwiches, salads, and simple entrees all day long. Tables on the patio facing Royal Poinciana are ideal for people watching. *Sun.–Thurs. 7a.m.–9p.m., Fri.–Sat. 7a.m–10p.m. 221 Royal Poinciana Way, 561-832-0992. $$*

TREVINI RISTORANTE

This charming Italian restaurant opened in 2000 and, despite changing locations, has been a local favorite ever since. Dine at tables set around a fountain in the charming brick courtyard edged with tropical greenery, or step into the appealing, contemporary dining room, with beige walls and black and white accents and arched French doors looking out to the courtyard. The Italian owners have created a classic menu and the cuisine is delightfully authentic, from the prosciutto with melon to the pappardelle amatriciana, to the saltimbocca and the osso buco. Excellent wine list includes many fine Italian reds and a Franciacorta, Italy's sparkling wine created using the Champagne method. There's a curvy, comfortable bar. *Lunch 11:30a.m.–2p.m., dinner 5p.m.–10p.m. 290 Sunset Ave., 561-833-3883. $$$*

ELSEWHERE ON THE ISLAND
AL FRESCO

A delightful spot to have breakfast, lunch, and dinner. Located five miles south of Worth Avenue, this charming, casual restaurant has a splendid view of the Atlantic Ocean. It is set near the waters' edge at the Palm Beach Par 3, on the second floor of a charming two-story tropical-plantation-style building with a wraparound dining terrace open to the tropical breezes. Excellent choices include the fried calamari, the roasted portobello mushroom, and the lobster salad. The lunch menu features tasty sandwiches and soups, and the dinner menu offers a delicious selection of pizzas and pastas, plus fish, chicken, and veal entrees. Small dining room and handsome bar inside. Reservations not accepted for lunch. *Breakfast daily 7a.m.–10:30a.m., lunch daily 11a.m.–4p.m., dinner Mon.–Thurs. 4p.m.–9p.m., Fri.–Sun. 4p.m.–10p.m. 2345 S. Ocean Blvd., 561-273-4130. $$*

**THE CIRCLE
AT THE BREAKERS
Feel like splurging on brunch?**
This exquisite dining room at the Breakers Resort, with its stunning 30-foot-high, circular frescoed ceiling decorated with murals of Renaissance landscapes, is the setting for a pricey but luscious Sunday brunch: Bloody Marys, Belgian waffles, pasta dishes and omelets made to order, fresh fruits, and pastries galore.

GREAT STOPS FOR BREAKFAST AND SUNDAY BRUNCH

AL FRESCO
Sit outside on the second-floor terrace, relaxing over breakfast and enjoying the stunning ocean view, as the golfers below struggle on the 13th and 14th holes.

CAFÉ BOULUD
The spot for an elegant breakfast and a sumptuous Sunday brunch (Saturdays, too) indoors or outdoors on the delightful terrace.

GREEN'S PHARMACY
For a basic, old-fashioned coffee shop, nothing beats Green's.

SURFSIDE DINER
Coffee shop décor for sure, but the menu includes four versions of eggs Benedict, organic omelets, and unexpected items such as arugula and champagne.

TABOO
From Jupiter all the way south to Delray, this popular Sunday brunch stop is on everyone's radar, so be sure to make a reservation.

4.
BARS, ENTERTAINMENT, AND DANCING

Palm Beach has a number of excellent bars, several places to dance, and an outstanding cabaret show. The bars, which are all inside restaurants, are entertaining and full of character. They fill up at the end of the day and can be busy throughout the evening on Fridays and Saturdays. Not all have TVs, but the ones that do are indicated below.

Like restaurants in this book, the establishments below are organized by location, those on or near Worth Avenue and those on or near Royal Poinciana Way.

WORTH AVENUE AREA

BICE
This spot can be jam-packed, particularly on weekend evenings. Silenced TVs at each end of the bar are almost always set to sports. Also a small lounge area with sofas and chairs. *11a.m.–10:30p.m. 313 Worth Avenue, 561-835-1600.*

BRICKTOP'S

A casual, happening watering hole, which is actually made up of two bars facing each other, one outside and one in. Sit at the inside bar and you can watch the open-kitchen action via a giant mirror. Two large silenced TVs. Best espresso martinis on the island. *11a.m.–10p.m. 375 S. County Rd., 561-855-2030.*

BUCCAN

Totally crowded and totally trendy small bar popular with singles of all ages. Large, silenced TV usually set to sports. Entertainment Friday nights. *Sun–Thurs 5p.m.–11p.m., Fri–Sat 5p.m.–midnight. 350 S. County Rd., 561-833-3450.*

CAFÉ BOULUD

Classy, dark, and comfortable, this quiet cocktail lounge is perfect for a tête-à-tête or a genteel larger gathering. Inside the contemporary dining room is a large, three-sided convivial bar for eating and drinking. *11:30a.m.–11p.m. 301 Australian Ave., 561-655-6060.*

CAFÉ L'EUROPE

The long, elegant brass-railed bar in the Bistro room has comfortable high chairs and is a wonderfully romantic stop for cocktails before or after dinner. Piano music nightly and local celebrity pianist David Crohan plays September through June. Light bite bar menu available. *Tues.-Sun. 6:30p.m.–9:30p.m. (Closed Tuesday off-season). 331 South County Road, 561-655-4020.*

LEOPARD LOUNGE AT THE CHESTERFIELD HOTEL

Dramatically decorated with plenty of black lacquer,

granite, beveled mirrors, and a red R-rated ceiling, the Leopard Lounge is dazzling and one of a kind. A single large room contains the Leopard Lounge restaurant, a long U-shaped bar, an area of petite tables for cocktails (the ones way in the back are the quietest), and a small (and often quite crowded) dance floor. A great place to dance and people watch. Entertainment nightly starting at 5:30 p.m. Dance music starts about 8p.m. (although one can also dance to the cocktail time music). *Sun.-Thurs. 11:30a.m.–11p.m., Fri.–Sat. 11:30a.m.–midnight. 363 Cocoanut Row, 561-659-5800.*

POLO AT THE COLONY
Dancing to live music Tuesday through Saturday in season. On Friday nights crowds head here to dance to a live band playing the music of the Temptations, the Supremes, Marvin Gaye, and other Motown favorites. *Friday night Motown Night at the Colony Hotel begins at 9p.m. Cover charge. 155 Hammon Ave., 561-655-5430.*

ROYAL ROOM AT THE COLONY
The cabaret shows here are truly exceptional. The entertainers are among the best cabaret entertainers in the world and the setting is intimate and sophisticated. The room is so small and the star-studded entertainers so close to the audience that you could almost be at an elegant party in a private home. Reserve a table for dinner and the show or just come for the show. The line-up runs November through mid-April, with entertainers performing for one or two weeks, usually Tuesday through Saturday. Tremendous thanks go to Rob Russell, who masterminds these events. People dress up and jackets are required. There is also a summer cabaret program. *Dinner seat-*

49

ing begins around 6:30p.m. Seating for tables for show only is at 8p.m. 155 Hammon Ave., 561-659-8100.

TABOO
Around since 1944, this legendary spot has been visited over the years by many of the rich and famous. It has one of the most appealing bars in Palm Beach: long, dark, and comfortable, with a tank full of playful tropical fish in the middle, a small and silenced TV at either end, and Bobby, one of the best bartenders ever. The atmosphere is definitely neighborhood bar, although almost everyone who visits south Florida puts Taboo on his or her bucket list. Definitely come here at least once, for the legend, for the people watching, and for the drinks, including their fabulous martinis. *11:30a.m.–10:30p.m., later on weekends. 221 Worth Avenue, 561-835-3500.*

ROYAL POINCIANA AREA
CUCINA DELL'ARTE
This popular three-sided bar with a large TV stays busy well into the night. Bartenders head here after work for late night fun. *11a.m.-3a.m. 257 Royal Poinciana Way, 561-655-0770.*

HMF
Located in the fabulous Florentine Room in the main building of the famed Breakers resort, the elegant, frequently crowded HMF (for Henry Morrison Flagler) is an enormous, one-of-a-kind cocktail lounge. Definitely worth a visit, for the history, the fabulous bar scene, the ornate ceiling, and the atmospheric buzz. Dinner also served. *5p.m.–11p.m. One S. County Rd., 561-655-6611.*

MEAT MARKET

Appealing, somewhat glitzy bar plus a comfortable lounge area perfect for relaxing. Can be quite crowded on weekends. *Sun.–Thurs. 4p.m.–11p.m., Fri.–Sat. 4p.m.–midnight. 191 Bradley Place, 561-354-9800.*

PALM BEACH GRILL

One of the hottest bars on the island for Palm Beachers. The décor is classy but hard to see through the crowds who head here when the doors open and stay all evening. Bar and high-top tables for dining and drinking. High-energy and can be on the cacophonous side. Several silenced TVs. *Sun.-Thurs. 5p.m.-10p.m., Fri.-Sat. 5p.m.-11p.m. 340 Royal Poinciana Plaza, 561-835-1077.*

PB CATCH SEAFOOD AND RAW BAR

A comfortable bar and an inviting spot for a peaceful drink. There is one silenced TV. Also a delightful raw bar in the main dining room with the day's oyster specials scrawled on the backboard. *Mon.–Sat. 4:30p.m.–11p.m., Fri.–Sat. 4:30p.m.–midnight. 251 Sunrise Ave., 561-655-5558.*

SANT AMBROEUS

This chic bar is a classy stop for cocktails, although it can be a bit frenetic. The inventive drink menu incorporates lots of fresh fruits and juices. *Sun.–Thurs. 11:30a.m.–10p.m., Fri.–Sat. 11:30a.m.–11p.m., 300 Royal Poinciana Plaza, 561-285-7990.*

TREVINI

Small, comfortable curved bar with a silenced TV located at one end of a handsome dining room. *4p.m.-–11p.m., 290 Sunset Ave., 561-833-3883.*

TWO WORTH AVENUE
BAR-HOPPING WALKS
This area is perfect for a watering hole adventure.
It's delightfully easy to walk from place to place.

ELEGANT AND FESTIVE

Start with a cocktail or two at **Cafe l'Europe**, on the corner of South County Road and Brazilian. The setting is classy and the superb pianist David Crohan will play your favorite song. Next stop, **Café Boulud**. Walk west on Brazilian for one block, turn south on Hibiscus and continue a block to Australian. Then turn west to the entrance of the Brazilian Court and Café Boulud. Settle into chairs in the dark and spacious but intimate lounge. Finally, walk south along Hibiscus two blocks to Peruvian and turn right. A little more than halfway along the block is the via leading to **Renato's** gracious bar. On weekends there is delightful piano music.

BUSY AND CELEBRATORY

For crowds and a casual atmosphere, start with a drink at **Taboo's** bar on Worth Avenue just a few doors west of South County Road. Then walk east to South County Road and north one block to **Brick-Top's**, which has an inside and outside bar, and where you can get the best espresso martini on the island. Now head four blocks north to **Chez L'Epicier**, on the corner of South County Road and Royal Palm Way, and check out their fancy drink menu that includes a Bourbonade and a Bloody Bacon Caesar. Next stop is **Buccan**. Walk south on South County Road two blocks. If there's no room, head to the bar at **Bice**. Walk south two blocks to Peruvian, turn west and walk a block and a half, crossing Hibiscus.

5.
SANDWICHES, COFFEE, TAKEOUT, AND MARKETS

So you just want a sandwich, or maybe a cappuccino or an ice cream cone, or perhaps a bottle of Veuve Clicquot? You can find them all right here on the island. As in the restaurant chapter, the stores below are organized by their location, either in the Worth Avenue Area or the Royal Poinciana Area.

ON OR NEAR WORTH AVENUE
CAFE DELAMAR
This tiny, hidden take-away spot is worth visiting for inspired sandwiches and soups as well as delicious hot dogs. Daily specials might include a black forest ham, brie, and apple panini or a grilled chicken and cheddar salad. Two little tables outside. *Mon.–Sat. 9a.m.–3p.m. In the middle of Via DeMario (enter from 326 Peruvian or 325 Worth Avenue). Via Demario, #4 326 Peruvian Ave., 561-659-3174.* $

OCEAN SANDWICHES
This popular stop on the way to the beach is famous

for fabulous specialty hoagies, including the New York Style (turkey, ham, Swiss, coleslaw, and Russian dressing) and the Italian Combo (ham, Genoa salami, and provolone). Also sandwiches, traditional subs, chili, wraps, and salads. Take-out counter plus two little tables. *Mon.–Sat. 10a.m.–4p.m. Two and a half blocks north of Worth Ave. 363 S. County Rd., 561-655-7911. $*

PASTRY HEAVEN
There's something for everyone at this little bakery and sandwich shop: brewed coffee and cappuccino, croissants, tasty grilled panini, traditional sandwiches, salads, soups, sushi, and freshly-baked bread, cookies, and pastries. Cakes made to order. Four little tables inside, more in the courtyard. *Mon.–Sat. 8a.m.–4:30p.m. One and a half blocks north of Worth Ave., 375 S. County Rd., 561-655-0610. $*

PICCOLO MONDO
It's a take-out window, but this is the kitchen of well-known Renato's restaurant, and the menu includes hot and cold pasta dishes, Italian sandwiches (meatball, chicken parmigiana), and more traditional sandwiches (Reuben, club, tuna salad). A great place to pick up picnic fare for the beach or for under a banyan tree overlooking the Town Docks. *At the rear (north) end of Renato's restaurant, corner of Peruvian Ave. Mon.–Sat., 11a.m.–3p.m. 87 Via Mizner, 561-655-9599. $*

SANDWICH SHOP AT BUCCAN
As you'd expect, Buccan's small take-away menu perfects the unexpected — sandwiches include steak tartare and arugula tucked in crusty bread, roast pork with broccoli rabe and provolone, BLT with arugula,

smoked yellowfin tuna salad, and Banh Mi-eatball. Don't miss the homemade potato chips (in those little brown bags on the counter). Also cookies baked daily. Takeout only. *(Despite address, actually on Australian Ave. Walk along Australian Ave. past Buccan to second set of doors after iron gate). Daily 11a.m.–3:30p.m. 350 S. County Rd., 561-833-6295. $*

STARBUCKS
Practically everyone knows Starbucks, but for those just arriving from another planet, this is the place to come for cold and hot coffee drinks galore (cappuccinos, lattes, frappuccinos, espressos, and more) plus smoothies, biscotti, and a small selection of sandwiches, salads, and snacks. *Mon.–Sat. 8a.m.–8p.m., Sun. 8a.m.–7p.m. 150 Worth Ave., #110 (in the courtyard just east of Saks Fifth Avenue), 561-651-7740. $*

SURFSIDE DINER
This spot looks and sounds just like a comfortable, old-fashioned coffee shop, with tables, booths, and a large U-shaped counter for dining, accompanied by the clatter of china and silverware. The menu matches the ambience, with some surprises tucked here and there, like arugula, organic eggs, a Power Start smoothie, and champagne. Come here for blueberry pancakes, eggs Benedict four ways, patty melts, giant salads, grilled shrimp with avocado, burgers, hot dogs, great fries, and classic milk shakes. *Daily 9a.m.–3p.m. Four blocks north of Worth, 314 S. County Rd., 561-659-7495. $*

ON OR NEAR ROYAL POINCIANA WAY
GREEN'S PHARMACY
This Palm Beach landmark opened in 1938, and, except for prices, not much has changed since then. One

end of this drugstore is given over to a coffee shop/luncheonette. Squeeze your way onto a seat at the counter or sit at a formica-top table. Traditional coffee shop menu, large portions, speedy service. *7a.m.–4p.m. 151 N. County Rd., 561-832-0304. $*

ISLAND BEE
Umbrella tables mark the entrance to this casual and charming spot for a large selection of healthy acai bowls, smoothies (plus a choice of over 30 smoothie boosters), cold pressed juices, and coffees and teas. *Sun.–Thurs. 7a.m.–4p.m., Fri.–Sat. 7a.m.–midnight. 261 Royal Poinciana Way, 561-619-3657. $*

PATRICK LÉZÉ
This authentic French bakery is the place to come for yummy-looking, fresh-from-the-oven offerings including éclairs, napoleons, cream puffs, quiches, croissants, macarons, and tortes. Also coffees, sandwiches, and salads. Several little tables outside. *Mon.–Sat. 7:30a.m.–4p.m. 229 Sunrise Ave., 561-366-1313. $*

SPRINKLES ICE CREAM & SANDWICH SHOP
There's nothing like a double-scoop ice cream cone with sprinkles on top to make you feel decidedly wicked. Tubs of ice cream showcase many flavors. Also light fare, and burgers. Couches and chairs inside and some tables outside. *Sun.–Thurs. 10a.m.–10p.m., Fri,–Sat.– 10a.m.–11p.m. 279 Royal Poinciana Way, 561-659-1140. $*

TOOJAYS
This classic Jewish deli turns out delicious versions of just what you would expect: thick sandwiches of hot corned beef or pastrami, chopped chicken liver, latkes, knishes, blintzes, and matzo ball soup. Also salads,

burgers, tuna melts, and a traditional turkey dinner. Take-out section and large casual dining room. *Daily 8a.m.–8p.m. 313 Royal Poinciana Plaza, 561-659-7232. $*

MARKETS (WITH PREPARED FOOD)
AMICI MARKET

Famous for its ultra-healthy made-to-order juice blends, smoothies, and açai and pitaya bowls (created by shop owner Mauricio), Amici is also an excellent stop for takeout, whether you are looking for a sandwich or a complete dinner for four. Come here for whole or by-the-slice pizza, calzones, meatball subs, fresh mozzarella and tomato, cold sandwiches, and burgers, plus an ever-changing selection of hot and cold prepared dishes, such as grilled salmon, chicken piccata, prime rib, corn on the cob, beet salad, quinoa salad, and more. Also a market, featuring top-quality beef, fresh fish, imported pastas and oils, fresh fruits and vegetables, and breads. Good wine selection. *Mon.–Sat. 8a.m–8p.m. (7p.m. off-season). 155 N. County Rd., 561-832-0201.*

C'EST SI BON

Reliably gourmet describes the delicious offerings here, whether you are searching for fine cheeses, nuts, crackers, teas, jellies, caviar, wines, champagne, cookies, or upscale take-out meals. Certain prepared foods — including beef tenderloin, turkey breast, poached salmon, egg salad, tuna salad, and quiche — are always available. In addition, there is an extensive list of specials that change daily and might include veal scallopine marsala, red pepper meatloaf, coconut-crusted jumbo shrimp, grilled lamb chops, plus hot and cold vegetable preparations and an array of creative salads. Custom gift baskets and catering services are also available. *Mon.-Fri. 9a.m.–6p.m., Sat. 9a.m.–5p.m. (3p.m. off-season). 280 Sunset Ave., 561-659-6503.*

PUBLIX SUPER MARKET
The only supermarket on the island, Publix can be hard to find because it is surrounded by tall, decorative hedges. It is a large, full-service supermarket that includes a deli, meat and seafood counters, prepared meals, and an extensive selection of wines from around the world. Also, valet parking. Only in Palm Beach, right? *6:30a.m.–10p.m. (sometimes shorter hours off-season). 135 Bradley Pl., 561-655-4120.*

Note: There are two liquor stores on the island. See page 104.

Evening Walking
Along Worth Avenue

Wherever you are staying, be sure to enjoy the pleasure of an evening spent walking along Worth Avenue. It is an ideal spot for a nighttime stroll. Embrace the ocean breezes, marvel at the starlit sky, enjoy the sparkly lights, and admire the beautiful window displays.

You can walk to cocktails and to dinner at the many bars and restaurants, to the beach, to dancing at the Chesterfield Leopard Lounge and the Colony Polo Bar, to the lake with its view of the West Palm Beach skyline.

If you are a guest at the Chesterfield or the Colony or the Brazilian Court, then just head out the door. If you are farther afield, then Uber or taxi to one end of Worth Avenue.

6.
EVENTS AND
ACTIVITIES

*Lectures, concerts, art exhibits, special events —
there are many, many organized activities going
on in Palm Beach. To find out what is happening
week to week, be sure to check out the "Spotlight:
Guide to Arts & Entertainment" section in the
Friday edition of the* Palm Beach Daily News.
*(May through September Spotlight appears in
the last Thursday edition of each month.)*
*Some of the events described below are free and
others require reservations and a ticket purchase. Prices are generally quite reasonable.*
*The following chapter covers events held just
once a year.*

LISTEN TO OUTSTANDING CHAMBER MUSIC
Internationally renowned chamber groups perform
January through March in an intimate and elegant
setting at the Flagler Museum. Following each concert, guests can meet the musicians during a champagne and dessert reception. *The Flagler Museum
Music series. Call 561-655-2833 for information.*

ATTEND A LECTURE

In February and early March, attend one or more of the Whitehall lectures at the Flagler Museum on Sunday afternoons. Each year the lecture series focuses on a specific theme, and some lectures are followed by a book signing. Can be viewed free online. *Call 561-655-2833 for information.*

GO TO A MOVIE

From mid-December through March the Society of the Four Arts offers the Friday Film Series. Movies are shown at 2:30p.m., 5:15p.m., and 8p.m. *Call 561-655-7226 for information.*

MEET AUTHORS AND JOIN BOOK DISCUSSIONS

From September through April the Society of the Four Arts holds two book-related series. Florida Voices features well-known Florida authors. In Talk of Kings, participants discuss a new title each session. Both events take place in the King Library. *Call 561-655-2766 for information.*

TAKE PART IN A LECTURE OR A WORKSHOP

From November through April, Campus on the Lake, sponsored by the Society of the Four Arts, offers lectures, workshops, classes, and field trips for almost every interest — flower arranging, photography, antiques, art history, architecture, literature, wine tastings, watercolor, music, computers, and more. Most of the events are held in the Fitz Eugene Dixon Educational Building. *Call 561-805-8562 for information.*

ENJOY MUSIC AND OLD MOVIES

Go see movies from the past at the historic Paramount Theater. Movies are shown on the first Thursday of the month, from December through May, at 7 p.m. Beforehand, there's a half hour of live musical entertainment, such as a performance by a jazz quartet. Music starts at 6:30p.m. Be sure to arrive early to check out the display of fabulous photos documenting more than half a century (1927-1980) of glamorous movie stars mingling with high society at Paramount Theater events. *Call 561-835-0913 for information.*

LEARN ABOUT THE CHURCH OF BETHESDA-BY-THE-SEA

Join the Church Lecture Tour to find out about the architecture and history of the Church of Bethesda-by-the-Sea. It begins at 12:15 p.m. every second and fourth Sunday of the month from September through May. Other months the tour is on the fourth Sunday at 11:15 a.m. *Call 561-655-4554 for information.*

EXPERIENCE HIGH TEA

Have High Tea in the Café des Beaux-Arts at the Flagler Museum. Available mid-November to mid-April. Special events on Valentine's Day and Mother's Day. *Call 561-655-2833 for information.*

SAVOR A WINE TASTING DINNER

Make reservations to join an elegant four-course dinner pairing cuisine with specially selected wines at Café Boulud. Wine dinners are held monthly and feature upscale wines and champagnes from around the world. *Call 561-655-6060 for information.*

FOCUS ON ARCHITECTURE

The Preservation Foundation, organized to preserve the historical and architectural heritage of Palm Beach, offers interesting lectures and book signings during the season. *Call 561-832-0731 for information.*

61

PALM BEACH
HAPPY HOURS

WORTH AVENUE AREA

Bice. 4p.m.–6p.m. Reduced price drinks and bar menu of half price appetizers and pastas.

BrickTop's. 4p.m.–6p.m. Well drinks and specialty drinks half-price and special bar menu items $8.

Buccan. Mon.–Fri. 4p.m.–7p.m. Half-price drinks, wine, and champagne.

Café Boulud. 4p.m.–6p.m., plus 10p.m.–midnight Fri.–Sat. Many drinks half price.

Chesterfield Leopard Lounge. Sun.-Thurs. 4:30p.m.–6:30p.m. Reduced price drinks and bar snacks.

Chez L'Épicier. 4:30p.m.–6:30p.m. Half-price drinks, wine, and champagne, and bar snacks.

Taboo. 4p.m.–6:30p.m. plus Sun.–Thurs. 9p.m.–11p.m. Half price martinis, wines, champagne, specialty drinks and special bar menu.

ROYAL POINCIANA WAY AREA

Cucina Dell' Arte. 5p.m.–10p.m. $5 wine, $3 beer, $12 Veuve Clicquot plus bar snacks.

Meat Market. 5p.m.–7p.m. Menu of half-priced drinks and reduced-price appetizers.

Nick and Johnnie's. 4p.m.–6:30p.m. Reduced price bar menu for drinks and food.

PB Catch. 4:30p.m.–6:30p.m. 2 for 1 oysters and drinks plus a $5 bar bites menu.

Note: Happy hours prices are generally honored only at the bar.

7.
ONCE-A-YEAR
EVENTS

If you are lucky enough to be in Palm Beach during any of these months, here are some fun things to do.

JANUARY
MINGLE WITH FERARRIS

Usually held on the third or fourth weekend in January, the Cavallino Classic attracts some of the rarest Ferraris in the world. Events include private and public racing at the Palm Beach International Raceway on Wednesday, Thursday, and Friday. On Saturday the Concorso di Eleganza is a daylong showcase of around 150 Ferraris parked on the lawn of The Breakers resort. An added benefit of this weekend is that car aficionados arrive in Palm Beach, many driving exotic cars; Worth Avenue and nearby streets are lined with stunning Ferarris, Bugatis, Lamborghinis, and other luxury sports cars. *Call 561-994-1345 for information.*

MARCH
VISIT ELEGANT HOMES AND GARDENS

Every year on the first Sunday in March the Garden Club of Palm Beach sponsors the Tour of Homes. Participants are invited into private homes and gardens. Tickets sell out fast, so be sure to reserve in advance. *Call 561-837-6635 for information.*

CREATE AMAZING HATS

In March, bring your children to the Mad Hatter's Tea Party and spend the morning fashioning festive bonnets and top hats. Parents and children then wear their new creations as they listen to a story from *Alice and Wonderland* and have tea in the Café des Beaux-Arts. *At the Flagler Museum. Call 561-655-2833 for date and information.*

SHOP AT THE HOUSE AND GARDEN DAY FAIR

The first Sunday in March — the day of the Garden Club Tour of Homes — the Society of the Four Arts holds an outdoor "fair" on the Four Arts lawn, called House and Garden Day. Everything from tablecloths to hats to carved wooden platters to orchids is for sale. *Call the Society of the Four Arts, 561-655-7226, for information.*

GO TO A PET PARADE

Every March the Worth Avenue Association holds the Pet Parade and Contest in Via Amore off Worth Avenue. Dogs, cats, and even bunnies of all sizes and shapes are dressed in an astonishing array of creative costumes and there are always winners in several categories. *Call the Worth Avenue Association, 561-659-6909, for date and information.*

MARCH OR APRIL
JOIN AN EASTER EGG HUNT

Bring your children and hunt for more than 8,000 eggs at the fabulous Easter Egg Hunt on the lawn of the Flagler Museum. Before the hunt, children can have their faces painted, be photographed with the Easter bunny, and play games. Bring your own baskets. *Call 561-655-2833 for date and information.*

APRIL
ENJOY AN AFTERNOON OF BLUEGRASS
In April, bluegrass musicians come to the Flagler Museum for the Bluegrass in the Pavilion concert. *Call 561-655-2833 for date and information.*

JUNE
HAVE A FREE DAY AT THE FLAGLER MUSEUM
Every June 5, on Founder's Day, the Flagler Museum's first floor and Henry Flagler's private railroad car are open to the public free of charge. *Call 561-655-2833 for information.*

JULY
WATCH DAZZLING FOURTH OF JULY FIREWORKS
Fireworks are set off from barges on Lake Worth just north of the Royal Park Bridge once darkness settles. Find a comfortable spot to stand along the water or on a bridge. Also, be sure to look north and south and west to catch the distant fireworks displays in surrounding towns.

SHOP SENSATIONAL SALES
Sales begin in late April and continue through July, but the best are in early July when final sales are everywhere. Look for discounts of 70 to 80 percent. There are smaller sales in January. Saks and Neiman-Marcus usually offer extraordinary bargains in July.

65

SEPTEMBER
JOIN FAMILY ACTIVITIES ON
GRANDPARENTS DAY

On Grandparents Day, the Flagler Museum provides fun for families in the Flagler Kenan Pavilion. Create a scrapbook page or a family tree. *Call 561-655-2833 for date and information.*

OCTOBER
PARTICIPATE IN A CHILDREN'S
HALLOWEEN COSTUME CONTEST

Children dress up in fabulous costumes for the Worth Avenue Association Halloween Costume Contest, held in Via Amore, just off Worth Avenue. *Call the Worth Avenue Association, 561-659-6909, for information.*

DRESS UP FOR A HALLOWEEN PARTY
FOR ADULTS

Join in the fun at Cafe l'Europe for a Halloween evening of revelry and devilry at this fabulous costume party. Includes a costume contest and prizes, of course! *Call 561-655-4020 for information.*

NOVEMBER
RACE IN THE THANKSGIVING 5K
TURKEY TROT

Run in the Town of Palm Beach United Way 5K Turkey Trot held on Thanksgiving Day. Age groups go from 9 and under to 70 plus. Some participants wear elaborate Thanksgiving Day costumes. Call early as tickets sell out fast. *Call 561-655-1919 for information*

LATE NOVEMBER OR EARLY DECEMBER
WORTH AVENUE CHRISTMAS
TREE LIGHTING

The Worth Avenue Association sponsors this ultra-popular Christmas Tree Lighting, which normally takes place the first Tuesday after Thanksgiving. Worth Avenue is closed to vehicular traffic, shops stay open late and offer light snacks and wine, and it seems as if the whole island shows up for the event. Santa and his elves lead a parade prior to the tree lighting. *The tree is located at the intersection of Worth Avenue and Hibiscus Avenue, and lights go on promptly at 6:29p.m. Call the Worth Avenue Association, 561-659-6909, for date and information.*

DECEMBER
FLAGLER MUSEUM CHRISTMAS TREE LIGHTING

The annual Christmas Tree Lighting at the Flagler Museum occurs in early December. Santa Claus stops by, there are choir performances and refreshments, and music is played on the original 1,249-pipe organ and the 1902 Steinway grand piano. *Call 561-655-2833 for date and information.*

SEND A LETTER TO SANTA

Want to reach Santa at the North Pole? Children can drop off their letters at the Flagler Museum on certain days in early December. They will receive free admission to the museum on the day of their letter drop off and must be accompanied by an adult. *Call 561-655-2833 for dates and information.*

ATTEND A PERFORMANCE OF THE *MESSIAH*

The Masterworks Chorus of the Palm Beaches offers a stunning performance of the *Messiah*, Handel's immortal masterpiece, at the Royal Poinciana Chapel in mid-December. *Call 561-845-9696 for date and more information.*

67

TAKE A NIGHTTIME TOUR OF WHITEHALL

Once a year, on the eve of the Christmas Tree Lighting, there is a tour of the Whitehall Mansion (the Flagler Museum), lighted by the original 1902 light fixtures. Christmas music and light refreshments are included. *Call 561-655-2833 for date and information.*

SEE SENSATIONAL NEW YEAR'S EVE FIREWORKS

Every New Year's Eve the Flagler Museum holds a fancy private party that includes a fabulous midnight fireworks display. The fireworks are visible from the Town Docks, the Lake Trail, and, to some degree, from almost anywhere between Worth Avenue and Royal Poinciana Way.

FUN THINGS TO DO

❧Head to Midtown Beach at dawn. The colors of the water and sky can be spectacular, as can the cloud formations.

❧Go back to the beach around dusk and watch day turn into night.

❧Take a drive up and down the island. (Beware of dead ends.)

❧Take a picnic to the park facing the Town Docks. Bring a blanket and set up on the grass, or find a bench under one of the banyan trees.

❧Walk through the Philip Hulitar Sculpture Garden at the Society of the Four Arts.

8.
EXPLORING PALM BEACH

Palm Beach is a charming place to explore. There are interesting historic sights including an extraordinary museum, inviting cultural activities, and beautiful parks and gardens. Frequently, when you are sitting on a bench, or walking into a park, or visiting a sight, you will see a little sign indicating that something — a bench, a fountain, even a building — is a gift. Much of what you see and visit in Palm Beach is there, in part, because of the generosity of Palm Beach residents and people who hold Palm Beach dear to their hearts.

MUSEUMS, SIGHTS, AND
CULTURAL ACTIVITIES
THE CHURCH OF BETHESDA-BY-THE-SEA

This graceful and majestic Episcopal church is set back from the road, making it easy to experience the full grandeur of its cast-stone Gothic-Spanish design. Inside, stunning stained glass windows illuminate the vaulted sanctuary. Follow the arched walkway to Cluett Memorial Garden, an exquisitely serene two-tiered oasis. Relax on a bench in the lower Tea Garden, then walk along the narrow pool and watch the carp vie for your attention. For shaded seating, head to the higher Color Garden and the two gazebos at the north end. The story of this church began in 1889, with the establishment of an Episcopal mission. To learn more about the architecture and history, join the Church Lecture Tour at 12:15 p.m. every second and fourth Sunday of the month from September through May. In June, July, and August the tour is monthly, on the fourth Sunday at 11:15 a.m. Concerts, choral services, and First-Sunday Evensongs are held throughout the year, and there is an appealing shop. Visitors are always welcome. *Shop closed Tues. and Sat. 141 S. County Rd., 561-655-4554.*

FLAGLER MUSEUM
This magnificent, must-see museum began as a wedding present. In 1902, Henry Morrison Flagler (who made his first batch of money as a founder of Standard Oil, then increased his fortune by masterminding the development of Florida via his railroad) built a 75-room, 100,000-square-foot mansion, known as Whitehall, for his wife as a wedding gift. This mega-mega-mansion completely dwarfs normal Palm Beach mega-mansions and is a glimpse into a grand way of life lived more than a century ago. Tour the museum, which is listed on the National Register of Historic Places, self-guided or with a docent. In-season there are art exhibits, concerts, and seasonal events (a Christmas tree lighting, an Easter egg hunt, and so on). And don't miss taking a walk through the historic and elegant railroad car, which was Flagler's private ride. It's in the Café des Beaux Arts, where you can also stop for lunch or afternoon tea in-season. Excellent gift shop. *General admission (tickets available*

on-line) $18 adults, $10 ages 13–17, $3 ages 6–12, under 6 free; includes tours and parking. 1 Whitehall Way, 561-655-2833.

PARAMOUNT THEATER BUILDING
Designed by Joseph Urban (who had a hand in designing Mar-a-Lago, Marjorie Merriweather Post's landmark estate and now a private club) in 1926 and listed on the National Register of Historic Places, this was once the famous Paramount Theater, built to be the most exclusive "picture house" in America. Between 1927 and 1980, more than 2,000 first-run films hit the screen here, and showings were a high-society event. Now it is home to a church, an art gallery, and assorted shops. Old movies are shown here on the first Thursday of the month, December through May. The glamorous days of old are documented in an excellent exhibit of movie posters and photographs of the movie stars and the rich and famous who came here to be entertained. *Free. 139 N. County Rd., 561-835-0913.*

ROYAL POINCIANA CHAPEL
Henry M. Flagler built this chapel at the south edge of his mansion, Whitehall (now the Flagler Museum) as a nondenominational chapel for his guests. It remains a nondenominational church, with services on Sundays. *Free. 60 Cocoanut Row, 561-655-4212.*

SEA GULL COTTAGE
This is the cottage Henry M. Flagler built as his winter home while he waited for Whitehall to be finished. It's the oldest house on the island. Although the inside is closed to the public, the building is worth a visit to see the stained glass windows, the landscaping, and the Queen Anne-style architecture. *On the west side of the Royal Poinciana Chapel. 60 Cocoanut Row.*

TOWN HALL AND THE MEMORIAL FOUNTAIN PLAZA

South County Road splits into separate northbound and southbound lanes between Brazilian Avenue and Chilean Avenue to make way for the beautifully restored Town Hall and the Memorial Fountain Plaza. The Town Hall dates from 1924, was redesigned by noted architect John Volk in 1967, and, thanks to the Preservation Foundation, was given an award-winning restoration in 1990 by architect Jeffery Smith. Inside are local government offices. Just north of the Town Hall, the Memorial Fountain Plaza has a small park, a reflecting pond, and a fountain designed by Addison Mizner and inspired by the Fountain of the Sea Horses at the Villa Borghese in Rome. *S. County Rd. between Brazilian Ave. and Chilean Ave.*

THE SOCIETY OF THE FOUR ARTS

Founded in 1936, the Society of the Four Arts (drama, music, art, and literature) is a remarkable cultural destination, offering from October through April a dazzling assortment of art exhibits, concerts, lectures, workshops, classes, field trips, and children and teen programs, as well as Metropolitan Opera and National Theater Live simulcast productions, a Friday Film Series, and the distinguished Esther B. O'Keeffe Speaker Series on Tuesday afternoons. All events are open to the public, and many require reservations and ticket purchase. (Tickets for the Tuesday Speaker series are reserved for members only until 15 minutes before the event, at which point any remaining tickets are available for purchase by the public.) Check the website (*fourarts.org*) for a full schedule of activities and to register or purchase tickets. The gardens and libraries are open year round and are free. *Entrance to the Four Arts Plaza is from Royal Palm Way. Driving east (to-*

ward the ocean) very first left after crossing the bridge over Lake Worth. Driving west (toward the mainland) last right before crossing the bridge over Lake Worth. 2 Four Arts Plaza, 561-655-7226.

THE FOUR ARTS CHILDREN'S LIBRARY
THE SOCIETY OF THE FOUR ARTS

This library is a charming and inviting venue for children to browse books, use computers, view exhibits tailored for them, and listen to stories. From October through April, the library offers story-time programs for preschool children (4 years and younger) most Mondays and Thursdays at 10:30 a.m., Family Story Time (8 years and younger) two or three Saturdays a month, and occasional field trips and classes for children kindergarten and older. Newborns through age 17 are welcome provided they are chaperoned by an adult (and adults are welcome, provided they are with a child). *Free. Second floor of the John E. Rovensky Administration Building. 2 Four Arts Plaza, 561-655-2776.*

THE GIOCONDA AND JOSEPH KING LIBRARY
THE SOCIETY OF THE FOUR ARTS

Designed in 1936 by architect Maurice Fatio, this was the initial building and headquarters of the Society of the Four Arts. Now it contains more than 75,000 books and periodicals, plus DVDs, CDs, an excellent Fine and Decorative Arts collection, and a rare-book room that includes the personal library and handmade scrapbooks of esteemed early-20th-century architect Addison Mizner. The appealing reading room is a perfect place to peruse today's newspapers, catch up on favorite periodicals, and browse through books. Book discussion groups are offered frequently from September through April. Call or check the website (*fourarts.org*) for the schedule. Some books are still referenced through an old-fashioned card catalog, which will stir up memories for those of a certain age. At the entrance to the building, be sure to take a look at the splendid murals by Albert Herter, depicting the four arts. *Free, with free WiFi. Borrowing privileges are available for a small annual fee. Mon.–Fri. 10a.m.–5p.m., Sat. 10a.m.–1p.m. Nov.–Apr. 3 Four Arts Plaza, 561-655-2766.*

PARKS AND GARDENS
BRADLEY PARK
The Lake Trail crosses this breezy, open expanse of grass, with the occasional tree, a dog water bar, and a clear view across Lake Worth to the skyline of West Palm Beach. *Northwest corner of Royal Poinciana at N. Lake Way.*

EARL E. T. SMITH PARK
Thanks to the Preservation Foundation, the town has this tiny and inviting rectangular park edged with thick tropical greenery, including trees that provide welcome shade. An oval ring of stone benches encircles a large fountain. During much of the year, the park is bedecked with cascading boughs of brilliant purple bougainvillea blossoms. *Just west of the Town Hall, at the northwest corner of S. County Rd. and Chilean Ave.*

LIVING WALL
Spearheaded by the Garden Club of Palm Beach, this dramatic 840-square-foot living wall is fabricated out of about 11,000 individual plants, all native to Florida and grouped by color to create a dramatic pattern. A computer-driven irrigation system keeps the plants

watered. *On the west wall of Saks Fifth Avenue. Esplanade, 150 Worth Avenue.*

MAYOR LESLY S. SMITH PARK
Less than a block north of Worth Avenue, this park is a fine place to sit and watch the activity on South County Road and at the post office across the street. It's small and shady, with a number of benches, as well as water for dogs. *Across from the post office, on the southwest corner of S. County Rd. and Peruvian Ave.*

PALM BEACH TOWN DOCKS PARK
This large grassy park east of the Palm Beach docks is a perfect spot to sit and view the yacht activity, gaze at the shores of West Palm Beach, and watch the Royal Park Bridge go up and down. A row of four banyan trees with overarching branches provides ample cover for the benches set underneath. Be aware that sometimes you may be sharing your seat with a line of ants on the move. *West side of S. Lake Dr., between Peruvian Ave. and Australian Ave., 500 Australian Ave.*

PAN'S GARDEN AT THE PRESERVATION FOUNDATION
It's hard to believe that not so many years ago this appealing oasis was the site of a parking lot and a derelict house. Thanks to the Preservation Foundation of Palm Beach, Pan's Garden, one of Palm Beach's most delightful parks, was created in 1994. Now mulch and pine needles cover paths that meander through 300 species of trees, grasses, shrubs, and wildflowers, all native to Florida. The park is only a half acre, but immensely peaceful. Check out the historic tile wall from the 1920s, rescued from the Casa Apava estate. A statue of Pan, the ancient Greek god of shepherds, faces a little gazebo, and benches are here and there.

75

Be sure to listen for the deep, throaty call of the bull-frogs that live in the pond at the north end. *Main entrance gate located on Hibiscus Ave. between Peruvian Ave. and Chilean Ave. Usually open Mon.–Fri. 9a.m.–5p.m., but hours can vary. Call 561-832-0731 for information.*

THE PHILIP HULITAR SCULPTURE GARDEN AND THE CHINESE GARDEN
THE SOCIETY OF THE FOUR ARTS

Located on the east side of the Four Arts Plaza, the Philip Hulitar Sculpture Garden is an exceptionally wonderful park, boasting a mixture of bougainvillea-covered pergolas, meandering paths, fountains and pools, an inviting and charming pavilion, shady benches (many donated), and a variety of perfectly placed sculptures. Look for Lawrence Holofcener's bronze of Winston Churchill and Franklin Roosevelt chatting (yes, the names on the sign are reversed) and the absolutely stunning *Recovery* by Grainger McKoy. Demonstration gardens, maintained by the Garden Club of Palm Beach, showcase Florida's many tropical plants. One of these areas, the Chinese Garden, is walled in, and the entrance is just south of the King Library. It's hard to believe that in 1965 this was an abandoned vacant lot. *Entrance to the gardens is just south of the King Library. Daily, 10a.m.–5p.m. (closed on major holidays). 3 Four Arts Plaza.*

THE SOCIETY OF THE FOUR ARTS PLAZA

The Society of Four Arts buildings and gardens are all part of the plaza, which borders Lake Worth and is a pleasant spot for a stroll. Look for the striking, stainless steel Isamu Noguchi sculpture on the west end of the plaza, near the Lake Trail. *Four Arts Plaza, 561-655-7226.*

9.
SPORTS
AND SPAS

Palm Beach is full of opportunities for outdoor activities. There are superb public tennis courts, an outstanding par 3 golf course, delightful beaches, and excellent places to ride bicycles. You can even go paddleboarding with your dog. For an indoor activity, consider taking a fun dance lesson. And, to put yourself back together after all these activities, just head to a full-service spa.

BEACHES AND SWIMMING

The town of Palm Beach has two magnificent Atlantic Ocean beaches perfect for swimming, sunbathing, shelling, and walking. From late spring through early fall, the waters frequently match the brilliant turquoises and aquamarines seen in the Bahamas and the Caribbean. Be aware that strong waves here can have dangerous undercurrents, and it is advisable to use caution. Florida is the most important turtle nesting area in the United States, so during turtle season (May through October) be careful not to disturb turtle nests, which are marked with tape by volunteers who walk the beach daily at dawn.

MIDTOWN BEACH

Worth Avenue, Palm Beach's legendary shopping destination, leads straight to Midtown Beach. In fact, the
tall clock tower at the corner of Worth Avenue and
South Ocean Boulevard marks the juxtaposition of the
east end of elegance and the start of the sand. This is
a lovely white sand beach, often strewn with shells.
Despite re-nourishment, recent storms have carried
sand out a few hundred feet past the waterline (you
can see this out there when you swim). The main entrance is two blocks north of Worth Avenue, on South
Ocean Boulevard. Bring everything you need, as there
are no concessions. For take-out ideas, see page 53.
Also the nearby Sunoco gas station, at the corner of
Australian Avenue and South County Road, carries
sodas and snacks. *Restrooms located beneath sun-
ning and lookout area across from Chilean Ave. (follow ramp down to north side entrance). No
concessions. A simple outdoor rinsing shower at
beachside entrance to boardwalk. Main entrance on
S. Ocean Blvd. at Chilean Ave. (follow the switchback
boardwalk to the sand). Metered parking ($5 per
hour) along S. Ocean Blvd. For beach report (tides,
etc.) call 561-835-4693. 400 S. Ocean Blvd.*

PHIPPS OCEAN PARK

This delightful, wide white sand beach is four and a
half miles south of Worth Avenue. There are no concessions here, so be sure to bring with you everything
you might need. There are thatched-roofed areas for
shade, as well as tables, barbecue pits, and a large
parking lot. *Restrooms, showers. Metered parking
($5 per hour). 2100 S. Ocean Blvd.*

BICYCLES

Bikes are an excellent way to explore Palm Beach.

The Lake Trail (see page 94) is a six-mile, car-free paved walking trail that also accommodates bikes. It runs along the west side of the island from the Town Docks at Peruvian Avenue all the way to the north end. If you bike here, please respect those on foot. Also, the trail is for leisurely biking, not racing. Local hotels often have bicycles available for guests. Do be careful of traffic when riding along the major thoroughfares and note that despite the low speed limits and lack of hills, some roads are quite curvy and can be somewhat dangerous.

.
PALM BEACH BICYCLE TRAIL SHOP
Come here for a large supply of rental bicycles. The friendly and helpful staff can give you suggestions of where to bike and a useful, easy-to-follow bike trail map. *In-line skates also available. 223 Sunrise Ave., 561-659-4583.*

DANCING
PARAMOUNT BALLROOM DANCING
Spruce up your dancing skills or start from scratch. No experience or partner necessary. Group lessons and private lessons available. *211 Royal Poinciana Way, 561-832-2141.*

GOLF
PALM BEACH PAR 3
This Par 3 is a challenging and entertaining course (think lots of water and sand and thick stands of grass) in a spectacular setting, sandwiched between the Atlantic Ocean and the Intracoastal Waterway. It was originally designed by renowned golf course architect Dick Wilson and redesigned and renovated in 2009 by World Golf Hall of Fame champion Raymond Floyd. The 18 holes range from 81 to 211 yards. Also, a full-

length driving range, a putting green, private lessons, clinics, a pro-shop, and the always popular oceanfront Al Fresco restaurant (*see page 45*). *2345 S. Ocean Boulevard, 561-547-0598.*

Note: The Breakers resort golf courses are not included here because they are for hotel guests and members only.

PADDLEBOARD WITH YOUR DOG
SALTY DOG PADDLE
Take a paddleboard tour with your pet and explore the waters around Bingham Island, in the middle of Lake Worth. Access is from the Southern Boulevard Bridge, about two miles south of Worth Avenue. Go alone or with a group. Lessons are provided for beginners and life jackets and boards are available for dogs of all sizes. This is a volunteer organization and all proceeds go to animal rescues. Other tours also offered. *Office in Palm Beach but participants meet where tours begin. Call or text 561-777-5999.*

TENNIS
SEAVIEW PARK TENNIS CENTER
These seven beautifully maintained clay courts are just six blocks north of Worth Avenue and are lighted for night play. Shaded benches are situated between courts, and there is a small covered observation area, plus a practice wall and a small pro shop. Come here for open play and for private individual and group lessons, or sign up for clinics and mixers. Courts are busy in-season, so it's best to reserve in advance. *Hours 7:30a.m.–8p.m. 340 Seaview Ave., 561-838-5404.*

PHIPPS OCEAN PARK TENNIS CENTER
These six excellent clay courts are four and a half miles south of Worth Avenue, just off the Atlantic Ocean.

There is a shaded viewing area and a pro shop. Call to arrange for open play, private individual and group lessons, and clinics. Courts are not lighted, and they close at dusk during the season and often by 12:30 p.m. off-season. *Call for hours. Quite busy in-season. 2201 S. Ocean Blvd., 561-227-6450.*

Note: The Breakers resort tennis facilities are not included here because they are for hotel guests and members only.

SPAS

Whether you've spent the day biking around the island, playing the Palm Beach Par 3, or vegging out with a book you pretended to read, you're surely ready for a massage or a manicure or a foot treatment at a relaxing, full-service spa.

SPA AT THE BREAKERS

This large and luxurious (and quite pricey) spa offers a complete range of sumptuous beauty treatments. Come here for maniciures, pedicures, massages, hair cuts and blow drys, facials, and a variety of make-up services. There's an extensive menu for each type of service. Indoor and outdoor facilities. *One South County Rd., 877-724-3188.*

SPA CARA

With soothing, candlelit treatment rooms and professional personnel, this full-service spa boasts an extensive menu with a wide range of massages (including one for couples) and many types of facials, plus waxing, nail services, and, for an instant and gorgeous deep color Florida tan, custom air brush tanning. *283 Royal Poinciana Way, 561-868-7010.*

81

SPLENDID PALM
BEACH SIGHTS

Pelicans flying in formation
or diving for dinner.

Spectacularly gaudy sunrises and sunsets.

Sandpipers standing on one leg, looking
silly.

Dolphins playing in the ocean.

Night skies brilliant with stars and planets
and shooting stars and satellites.

The full moon, thrusting itself
out of the ocean.

Geckos running across the sidewalks.

Snowy white egrets, spreading their lovely
wings as they take to the air.

Fancy and delicate shells on the beach.

Adorable tiny dogs
walking their owners along Worth Avenue,
or peeking out of a Gucci handbag
in a fancy restaurant,
or hanging out of the driver's side window
of a passing car.

10.
ART GALLERIES

Visiting the art galleries along Worth Avenue is kind of like dropping into pop-up versions of the world's finest modern and contemporary art museums. You might see work by Damien Hirst, Pablo Picasso, Gerhard Richter, Jeff Koons, Keith Haring, Georgia O'Keeffe, Andy Warhol, Mark Rothko, among others. Lesser-known and emerging artists are also represented. Don't feel intimidated — everyone is welcome to step in and look. Just please don't touch anything, and please don't walk into a gallery carrying food or beverages. For those of you wondering what, really, is the difference between modern and contemporary art, the generally accepted answer is that modern art begins in the 1870s with the Impressionists and continues on until the 1970s, and contemporary art is from the 1970s up until right now.

ARCATURE FINE ART
This spacious, high-ceilinged gallery with broad stairs leading to a second-floor balcony is a perfect venue for the mostly late-modern and contemporary works shown here. It's possible to view outstanding works by

Helen Frankenthaler, Keith Haring, Damien Hirst, and Robert Motherwell, among others. *318 Worth Ave., 561-805-9388.*

BRINTZ GALLERIES
This inviting gallery is on South County Road, a block and a half north of Worth Avenue. It's easy to spot: look for the long row of windows showcasing knockout contemporary paintings. The focus here is on contemporary art by established and emerging artists. Brintz Galleries also represents the estate of Larry Rivers. *375 S. County Rd., 561-469-7771.*

DTR MODERN GALLERIES
Come here for a large selection of work by Hunt Slonem, famous for his fabulous birds and colorful butterflies, plus works by many other contemporary artists, some modern artists, and some emerging artists. Be sure to say hello to the friendly guard, who stands just inside the entryway. *Just south of Worth Ave. across from the Living Wall, 440 S. County Rd., 561-366-9387.*

GALLERY BIBA
Don't miss this enticing narrow gallery with a remarkable mixture of ultra-edgy and serene contemporary art. Lots of 3-D work, ranging from larger-than-life realistic swimmers, bling-bling hamburgers, and sparkly cans of Spam to exquisitely perfect, sculpted-marble ballet dancers and handbags. Also videos, awesome photographs, and dramatic art created with experimental painting techniques. It's a pleasure to visit here, where nothing is remotely ordinary. Be sure to check out the small upstairs display and the intimate backyard sculpture garden. *224A Worth Ave., 561-651-1371.*

GALLERY VIA VENETO

Charming, remarkably lifelike, bronze sculptures of children at play, some painted bright colors, are arranged outside this tiny gallery. Their creator is Prince Monyo (full name: Prince Monyo Mihailescu-Nasturel Herescu), born in Bucharest, Hungary. His bronzes are displayed in many cities in North America and Europe. *In Via Amore (middle entrance from Worth Ave.), just west of Cafe Flora. 250 Worth Ave., 561-835-1399.*

HOLDEN LUNTZ GALLERY

Photography is the focus here, and a wide range of well-known American and European photographers are featured. Subject matter runs the gamut, from fashion to photojournalism to still-life to experimental, using traditional and alternative (nonsilver) photographic processes. Exhibits change regularly. *332 Worth Ave., 561-805-8550.*

JOHN H. SUROVECK GALLERY

Follow Via Parigi into the courtyard to find this peaceful gallery, which specializes in American paintings, drawings, watercolors, and prints from the 19th and 20th centuries. Artists include Thomas Hart Benton, William Glackens, and many more. *8 Via Parigi, 561-832-0422.*

LIMAN GALLERY

Affordable art as well as rare and unusual books are the strong points here at this gallery, which is located about two miles north of Worth Avenue and two blocks north of Royal Poinciana Way. Several gallery rooms are devoted to paintings, drawings, vintage prints, posters, and mixed media, plus bins of matted art ready for framing. A back gallery room focuses on collectible magazines, coffee-table art books, and rare and unusual vintage books. *The Paramount Building, 139 N. County Rd., 561-659-7050.*

TAGLIALATELLA GALLERIES
A heavy hitter in the contemporary art world, Taglialatella specializes in pop art and street art, encompassing artists such as Warhol, Lichtenstein, Hirst, Frankenthaler, Basquiat, Wesselmann, and the fabulous Mr. Brainwash. Ask about their in-season lecture series. Galleries also in New York City and Paris. *Entrance is a short way into Via Bice. 313 1/2 Worth Ave., 561-833-4700.*

WALLY FINDLAY GALLERIES
Multiple rooms downstairs and upstairs showcase modern and contemporary artists and late-19th- and early-20th-century French artists. In addition, the frequent themed exhibits, such as Works on Paper, are always worth seeing. Wally Findlay was established in 1870. There is a gallery in New York City as well. *165 Worth Ave., 561-655-2090.*

FRAMING
PIERCE ARCHER
So you bought a beautiful piece of art and now want to get it framed or have it re-framed to fit with your decor. Well, there's no one better to go to than John Archer, a master at his craft. He has an eye for choosing the perfect frame — large or small — to enhance and bring out the best in a painting. Also provides custom frames and exceptional art restoration services. *235 Peruvian Ave., 561-623-7371.*

11.
SEVEN WALKS AROUND THE ISLAND

The island of Palm Beach is long and narrow, with many places perfect for walking. It is just a little more than half mile from the Atlantic Ocean at the east end of Worth Avenue to the Town Docks on Lake Worth on the west side of the island. It's only a mile and a half between the two commercial areas of Worth Avenue and Royal Poinciana Way. All the streets and avenues in the ten-block area extending north from Worth Avenue have wide sidewalks. The Lake Trail runs along the west side of Palm Beach from the Town Docks all the way to the north end of the island.

Below are five suggestions for fun, self-guided walks. All can be reversed, if the ending point is actually a more convenient starting point. And, of course, you can make up your own routes. Also below are two guided Worth Avenue Walking Tours, one historical and one about ghosts. If you walk yourself silly, remember, you can al-

ways relax afterwards with a massage at Spa Cara (see page 81).

SELF-GUIDED WALKS
WALK #1: A SHOPPING STROLL — EXPLORING WORTH AVENUE AND THE VIAS

Worth Avenue is a charming street for a stroll, whether you are a window looker or a shopper extraordinaire. Here and there along Worth Avenue, walkways, called vias by the locals, lead off the avenue to enchanting, quiet courtyards that are wonderful places to explore. They are architecturally beautiful, offer places to sit, and are lined with interesting shops.

Most shops along Worth Avenue open at 10 a.m., but if you arrive a little earlier, you'll catch sight of shopkeepers polishing the doorknobs and sweeping the sidewalks in preparation for the day. It is a quaint experience and one of the ways Palm Beach can feel like a small town. This walk starts at the Clock Tower, on the east side of South Ocean Boulevard.

1. After taking pictures of yourself with the Clock Tower, cross over to Worth Avenue and begin the walk. The first via on Worth Avenue is in the Esplanade Courtyard. Take the first entrance after the parking lot driveway and follow it into the courtyard. Now you have two levels of shops to explore. There are several stairways and an elevator to the second level. You also might want to stop at Starbucks for a cappuccino or a latte and then settle at a courtyard table and do a little people watching.

2. Now follow the courtyard west to Saks Fifth Avenue, exit to Worth Avenue through the walkway or through Saks, then stay on the south side and walk west to the corner of South County Road. Take a look at the Living Wall, the verdant vertical garden adorning the west side of Saks Fifth Avenue. This lush and colorful formation is made up of more than 11,000 plants. A computer system keeps them watered.

3. Next cross South County Road and stop at the window of the DTR Gallery. If you have any questions, feel free to ask the security guard just inside the door.

4. Now walk along either side of Worth Avenue, checking out the shop windows. Stop at Gallery Biba, at 224 Worth Avenue, and take a look at the remarkable sculptures and other contemporary artwork.

5. Just across the street, at 221 Worth Avenue, is the legendary Taboo restaurant, a Palm Beach landmark since 1941.

6. The next via, also on the south side of Worth Avenue, is called Via Amore. There are actually three walkway entrances here, all leading to a quiet and spacious courtyard with seating arrangements and walls draped in brilliant bougainvillea. You may hear locals refer to Via Amore as the Gucci Courtyard, because for many years Gucci (which is now in the 100 block of Worth Avenue, near Saks) was located here.

7. Take the middle entrance, between Kassatly's and Mystique of Palm Beach (both shops are at 250 Worth Avenue), and walk into the courtyard. Notice the Spanish architecture and the beautiful old bougainvillea plants climbing the walls. The second floors are mostly private apartments.

8. There are numerous shops to explore here. If you are a dog owner, Bibi's Doggy Boutique is for you. Marley's Palm Beach Collection is the place for casual clothing. Il Sandolo offers custom-made sandals. And don't miss the whimsical Sherry Frankel's Melangerie. And if it's lunchtime, stop in at Cafe Flora.

9. Exit at the western walkway, past Island Company and St. John, and return to Worth Avenue.

Walk along Worth Avenue on either side, window-shopping, until you come to Via Bice at 313 Worth Avenue, on the north side. This is an example of a via lined with shops that does not lead to a courtyard. It cuts through the block and ends at Peruvian Avenue, between the clothing store Cashmere Beach and the restaurant Bice. You might want to stop in the Taglialatella Galleries, whose specialty is contemporary art, or Maryanna Suzanna, for hand-painted Italian ceramics.

10. Retrace your steps back to Worth Avenue and continue walking west on either side of the street.

11. The next large via, on the north side of Worth Avenue, is Via Mizner, where there are two entrances. The eastern entrance is between Vilebrequin and 100% Lino. Follow the via to a small courtyard. Walk through the courtyard into the second via. Ahead of you is the entrance to the restaurant Pizza al Fresco. The house on the south side of Pizza al Fresco was originally the estate of legendary Palm Beach architect Addison Mizner. His studio was on the top floor and offered a splendid 360 degree view of Palm Beach. The building is still a private house.

12. There are two Italian restaurants here: Renato's, which is quite fancy, and the casual Pizza al Fresco. If you stop for lunch at Pizza al Fresco, walk to its south end and you will see the grave of Addison Mizner's pet spider monkey, Johnnie Brown. The other grave is for Laddie, the dog owned by the family who bought the estate from Mizner.

13. There is also a take-out window at Piccolo Mondo's at the Peruvian Avenue end of the via. You can stop and pick up lunch and go have a picnic at the park at the Town Docks at the west end of Peruvian.

14. If you still feel like walking, head back to Worth Avenue and turn right. Choose either side of the street.

15. The last via on Worth Avenue is Via Parigi, on the north side of the street at 347 Worth Avenue. Follow the via to art galleries, shops including the Blue Caribe Jewelry Shop, and a fountain with seating around it.

16. Back out on Worth Avenue, continue west. Cross Cocoanut Row and continue on Worth Avenue. There are no more shops. When you get to the lagoon on the south side of Worth Avenue, look back and you will see the exclusive Everglades Club and perhaps people engaged in a game of croquet.

17. Continue on to the Town Docks, find a seat, and take in the views of boats and magnificent yachts, the West Palm Beach skyline in the distance, and the middle bridge to the north, which opens for water traffic twice an hour.

WALK #2: A ZIGZAG HEDGE WALK TO THE BREAKERS

This walk takes you through the mostly residential area just north of Worth Avenue, with an occasional stop, and it can end at the Society of the Four Arts Philip Hulitar Sculpture Garden. But, if you want to continue walking, then follow the steps to the Breakers and the Flagler Museum. Note the magnificent hedges and meticulous plantings as you stroll.

1. Start at Chilean Avenue and the Town Docks. Walk east two blocks on Chilean Avenue, then take a right (south) on Hibiscus Avenue. The entrance halfway along the block takes you into Pan's Garden, a showcase of plants indigenous to Florida. Follow the paths, find a bench, sit and listen for the bullfrogs' bellowing from the pond. (*For more information about Pan's Garden, see page 75.*)

2. Now retrace your steps back to Chilean Avenue and continue east to South County Road. If you are a shopper, you might want to stop in the Church Mouse, on the corner of Chilean Avenue and South County Road. The Church Mouse is the queen of thrift shops, with everything from designer clothes for men and women to furniture and books.

3. Turn left (north) on South County Road, walk north one block to Australian Avenue, cross the grassy area just north of the beautifully restored Town Hall, and continue east on Australian Avenue to the ocean.

4. Walk north along South Ocean Boulevard one block to Brazilian Avenue, then turn left (west) and follow Brazilian Avenue back to South County Road. Cross South County Road and either explore the shops just to the north and south or continue straight, walking all the way to the Town Docks. Turn right (north) on South Lake Drive and walk north. Cross Royal Palm Way and follow the paved walkway until you see the pointed metal sculpture. You are now at the west end of the Society of the Four Arts Plaza. Walk east along the grassy park to the King Library, and just south of the library you will see the entrance to the Philip Hulitar Sculpture Garden (*see page 76 for detailed information*). This is a lovely garden to stroll around and to find a sheltered bench to relax on. While here you might want to stop in the King Library and check up on the day's newspapers or enjoy a magazine.

5. If you still have energy, you can zig and zag your way north for several more blocks. Walk north past the library to Seaview Avenue and continue east to the ocean; from there, go north one block to Sea Spray, walk west to the lake, then north a block and back east on Seabreeze Avenue, and so on. When you get as far north as Barton Avenue, walk to the corner of Barton Avenue and South County Road and head into the gardens behind the Church of Bethesda-by-the-Sea and relax in one of the shady gazebos.

6. Now head back out to South County Road and walk

north until you come to the main entrance (second stoplight) to The Breakers resort. Walk down this long and magnificent driveway to the grand entrance. Feel free to explore. The Breakers, built by Henry M. Flagler, opened in 1926, and is modeled after the Villa Medici in Rome. Notice the paintings on the ceiling of the resplendent lobby, created by 75 artisans brought from Italy. Shoppers will want to stop in the appealing stores just south of the entrance, including the excellent News & Gourmet shop, which carries a splendid selection of home décor items and gifts.

7. Now walk back out the main entrance and follow the driveway to South County Road. Walk one block south to Pine Walk and cross the street and follow Cocoanut Walk (street name changes from Pine to Cocoanut), the paved walkway that leads to the Flagler Museum (*for information see page 70*).

WALK #3: A BEACH WALK

The Palm Beach Midtown Beach is the perfect spot for a beach walk. Search for seashells, gaze at the waves, enjoy the enormous expanse of ocean and sky, and breathe in fresh, clean air that has been traveling across the Atlantic for over four thousand miles, from the Western Sahara. This is a great walk in almost any kind of weather. The ocean has multiple personalities, and can be as still as a lake or ferocious from wind. The sky can be a solid, magical deep blue or a pale blue or a steel grey. The sky can be full of clouds in spectacular formations. In the early morning, especially in the warmer months, a small line of white clouds often parades across the horizon. At dawn and dusk the reds and oranges can be so brilliant they look unreal. The beach in midtown is easily accessible from South Ocean Boulevard and one can walk north or south.

1. Head to the intersection of Chilean Avenue and South Ocean Boulevard. The main entrance to the midtown beach is here. Follow the zigzag ramp down to the sand.

2. You can walk in either direction. If you choose to head north, you can follow the beach for about a half a mile.

3. If you choose to walk south, you can continue for several miles.

You can also exit and enter this beach at the public walkways farther north at Brazilian Avenue and at Clarke Avenue. If you walk south from the Clock Tower along the beach, you will need to retrace your steps to leave the beach. The stairs you see south of the Clock Tower are private property. Bear in mind that the sand dunes, with or without vegetation, are quite fragile, so always stay on walkways to enter and exit the beach and never walk across the dunes.

WALK #4: THE LAKE TRAIL WALK

Water views, of course, are coveted and many of the large estates in Palm Beach front the ocean or face Lake Worth, and the land stretching to the water is private. However, amazingly, on the west side of the island a six-mile public trail runs along the water's edge, basically cutting through the backyards of many estates. From the Town Docks to the north end of the island, it is possible to stroll along the water on a paved path, taking in spectacular views of Lake Worth and the distant skyline of West Palm Beach on one side and, on the other side, numerous glimpses, through gates and hedges, of elegant estates. There are no facilities on this walk, so you might want to bring water.

If you want to walk the whole trail, start at the Town Docks, near Worth Avenue, where it begins. You can also easily pick up the trail at the Flagler Museum and at Bradley Park, which is just north of Royal Poinciana Way.

1. To start at the Town Docks, go to the west end of Peruvian Avenue, which is one block north of Worth Avenue. Look for the paved trail at the water's edge. Follow it north across Royal Palm Way. You will now be in the Society of the Four Arts Plaza. Note the large sculpture on the left. (*For information about the Society of the Four Arts, see page 72*).

2. Keep walking north, following the trail. Lake Worth is on your left, estates on your right. The trail continues north to the Flagler Museum. Note the enormous roots of the Kapok tree, just before you get to the museum.

3. You can stop and visit the Flagler Museum or have tea at the Café Beaux-Artes. (*See page 70 for more information about the Flagler Museum.*)

4. The trail continues north until Royal Poinciana Way. Cross Royal Poinciana Way and walk across Bradley Park to resume walking on the Lake Trail Walk. For food or something to drink, the Royal Poinciana Way area is the last place to stop if you are headed north. Patrick Lézé is a good choice for a cappuccino or a pastry. They are located at 229 Sunrise Avenue.

WALK #5: SELF-GUIDED ARCHITECTURAL WALKING TOUR OF MIDTOWN PALM BEACH

The Preservation Foundation of Palm Beach has prepared an excellent, detailed self-guided walking tour of important buildings throughout the entire midtown area. To download a copy, go to *palmbeachpreservation.org*

GUIDED WALKS
WALK #6: HISTORICAL WALKING TOURS OF WORTH AVENUE

Every non-holiday Wednesday morning from early December through late April, Rick Rose leads an informative walking tour of Worth Avenue, covering everything from the history of the architecture to stories of the high-society scene. The walk lasts about 75 minutes. *Meet at 11a.m. at 256 Worth Avenue at Via Amore, across from Tiffany & Co. No reservations. $10 per person. Call (561) 659-6909 for information.*

WALK #7: GHOSTS OF PALM BEACH

Try your hand at communicating with spirits on this unusual ghost tour along Worth Avenue. Guests can experiment with dowsing rods at "known" ghost-sensitive spots along the way. *Every Friday and Saturday at 8p.m. and often Sundays also, at 7:30p.m. Tour starts at the Living Wall on Worth Avenue. Call 561- 353-6658 for more information and reservations.*

12.
ACROSS THE BRIDGES, ON THE MAINLAND

This book is strictly about the island of Palm Beach. However, the city of West Palm Beach, on the mainland, directly across the Royal Park Bridge and the Flagler Memorial Bridge, has much to offer. Below is just a small sampling of what is available to explore and enjoy. Almost everything listed is about ten minutes or less from Worth Avenue by car.

ANN NORTON SCULPTURE GARDENS
Two acres of delightful gardens feature monolithic sculptures and include plants that attract native birds. Among the special events here is the fabulous Festival of Trees in early December. *2051 S. Flagler Dr., West Palm Beach. 561-832-5328.*

ARMORY ART CENTER
This outstanding art center offers numerous classes and workshops in jewelry, painting, printmaking, sculpture, fused glass, ceramics, and more, as well as

a rich assortment of exhibits, lectures, special events, and salons. *1700 Parker Ave., West Palm Beach. 561-832-1776.*

CITYPLACE

There's always something happening at CityPlace, a popular complex that includes Macy's plus numerous other shops, as well as bars, restaurants, and comedy clubs; a 20-screen movie theater plus IMAX; and offers special events and live entertainment. *700 S. Rosemary Ave., West Palm Beach, 561-366-1000.*

NORTON MUSEUM OF ART

The largest museum in Florida, the Norton includes extensive collections of American, European, Chinese, and contemporary art, plus photography. The popular Art After Dark program every Thursday evening features a mix of exhibits, entertainment, film, and more. *1451 S. Olive Ave., West Palm Beach, 561-832-5196.*

PALM BEACH DRAMAWORKS

This award-winning theater showcases provocative productions plus Dramalogue, a series of talks and Q&As with well-known producers, playwrights, and theater critics. Also, other educational events. *201 Clematis St., West Palm Beach. 561-514-4042.*

RAYMOND F. KRAVIS CENTER FOR THE PERFORMING ARTS

One of the premier performing art centers in the southeast, the Kravis Center presents Broadway shows, orchestras from around the world, the Miami City Ballet, the Palm Beach Opera, lectures, comedians, jazz, dance, cabaret, and much more. *701 Okeechobee Blvd., West Palm Beach, 561-832-7469.*

13.
WHERE TO STAY

This book is essentially a guide for what to do once you've arrived in Palm Beach. In case you have not yet decided where to stay, here's a brief look at what's around on the island.

NEAR WORTH AVENUE
PALM BEACH HISTORIC INN
Small, simple inn two and a half blocks north of Worth Avenue, just north of Chilean Avenue. *13 units. 365 S. County Rd., 561-832-4009.*

THE BRAZILIAN COURT HOTEL
Winner of numerous awards, this full-service, four-star hotel is nestled in tropical greenery. Flowerbeds and fountains decorate the spacious interior courtyards. Celebrity Chef Daniel Boulud's Café Boulud is located here. *Member of Leading Hotels of the World. 80 units. 301 Australian Ave., 561-655-7740.*

CHESTERFIELD PALM BEACH
A classy, upscale hotel that is part of the Red Carnation Hotel Collection and a member of the Small Luxury Hotels of the World. Built in 1926, it has stunning, individually decorated rooms (some of them are very small but all of them are lovely). *Pool and restaurant. 53 units. 363 Cocoanut Row, 561-659-5800.*

COLONY PALM BEACH

This iconic hotel opened in 1947 and is a Palm Beach landmark. Well-known decorator Carleton Varney recently turned the rooms into bouquets of bright color. *Pool and restaurant. 94 units, 6 villas. 155 Hammon Ave., 561-655-5430.*

NEAR ROYAL POINCIANA WAY
BRADLEY PARK HOTEL

Small, historic 1920s hotel landmarked by the Palm Beach Historical Society, a block north of Royal Poinciana Way and close to restaurants, bars, shops, and the beach. *Rooms plus suites with full kitchens. 32 units. 280 Sunset Ave., 561-832-7050.*

THE BREAKERS

This legendary, five-star resort is a magnificent oceanfront complex with bars and restaurants, golf courses, tennis courts, swimming pools, a shopping arcade, and a full-service spa. *500 units. One S. Country Rd., 877-724-3188.*

OUTSIDE OF TOWN BUT IN PALM BEACH
FOUR SEASONS RESORT PALM BEACH

Located about six miles south of town, but still on the island of Palm Beach, is the oceanfront resort. *210 units. 2800 S. Ocean Blvd., 561-582-2800.*

14.
FAQs

Q. Is there a Starbucks on the island?
A. *Yes, in the courtyard of the Esplanade, at 150 Worth Avenue. Entrances to the courtyard are to the east of Saks Fifth Avenue.*

Q. Where can I see famous people?
A. *You may see them anywhere. Many well-known people live in Palm Beach part-time and you may see them in shops or restaurants or walking along the street. It is considered good form not to bother them.*

Q. How far away is the nearest airport?
A. *The Palm Beach International Airport is less than five miles from Worth Avenue.*

Q. Where is the club that President Trump owns?
A. *President Trump owns the Mar-a-Lago Club, located at 1100 South Ocean Boulevard, which is less than two miles south of Worth Avenue. This is a private club.*

Q. How can I get a taxi ?
A. *Taxis are not allowed to roam for fares on the*

island of Palm Beach. You must call them. For a Yellow Cab, call 561-777-7777. Uber cars are also available.

Q. What kind of clothes do I need?
A. *Resort wear works all year long, but in the winter bring a sweater for chilly days. Dress codes have been severely relaxed in the last several years but in-season, in fancy restaurants, men often wear jackets or even suits and many women wear cocktail dresses or comparable attire. During the day most anything goes. If you are invited to a private club, bear in mind that blue jeans are never allowed.*

Q. Where can I park?
A. *See "Parking" page 104.*

Q. It looks easy to buy something fancy or unusual in Palm Beach, but supposing I need something ordinary, like the running shoes I forgot to bring?
A. *Well, one of the amusing aspects of Palm Beach is that you can purchase almost anything you don't need right here, without leaving the island. But for most necessities of life (a hammer, basic gym clothes), you must head to the mainland. If you are desperate for some item, try Publix Super Market or any of the island drugstores. They usually carry something that will do. Otherwise, head to Cityplace, two miles from Worth Avenue across the Royal Park Bridge.*

Essential Information

AIRPORT
Palm Beach International Airport is just under five miles from Worth Avenue on Palm Beach.

BANKS AND ATMS
BB&T. 125 Worth Ave., 561-653-5594.
Chase Bank. 285 Sunrise Ave., 561-833-1017.
TD Bank. 380 S. County Rd., 561-355-5311.
Wells Fargo Bank. 255 S. County Rd., 561-655-7111.

CHURCHES AND SYNAGOGUES
Church of Bethesda-by-the-Sea (Episcopal). 141 S. County Rd. 561-655-4554.
Palm Beach Orthodox Synagogue. 120 N. County Rd. 561-838-9002.
Royal Poinciana Chapel (Post-denominational). 60 Cocoanut Row. 561-655-4212.
St. Edward Roman Catholic Church. 144 N. County Rd. 561-832-0400.
Temple Emanu-El of Palm Beach. 190 N. County Rd. 561-832-0804.

DRUGSTORES
Fedco Pharmacy. 255 Sunrise Ave., 561-659-6713.
Green's Pharmacy. 151 N. County Rd., 561-832-4443.
Lewis Pharmacy. 235 S. County Rd., 561-655-7867.

GAS STATION
Gray's Sunoco. 340 S. County Rd., 561-655-6645.

LIQUOR STORES

Hamptons Wine and Spirits Palm Beach. 257 Royal Poinciana Way, 561-832-8368.
Scotti Wines & Liquors. 369 S. County Rd., 561-655-5480.

LOCAL NEWSPAPER

The *Palm Beach Daily News*, a charming small-town newspaper known locally as "The Shiny Sheet," is published daily on-season. Be sure to check it out, to find out what is happening around town and for information on sales and special events. (From the first Sunday in May through the first Sunday in October, the newspaper is published on Sunday and Thursday.) Available at the Classic Book Shop at 310 South County Road, the Palm Beach Book Store at 215 Royal Poinciana Way, and in vending machines around town.

PARKING

Parking rules vary from street to street and sometimes vary from space to space, so be sure to read the signs carefully and completely (one space might be restricted until 6 p.m., another until midnight). If in doubt, park elsewhere, as parking rules are strictly enforced. Time limits are also strictly enforced. Don't expect to be given leeway if you are five or ten minutes over. Parking tickets start at $60.

There is a parking lot on top of the Esplanade at 150 Worth Avenue (turn onto Worth Avenue from South Ocean Boulevard and take the second left). There is also the Apollo Parking Lot, just north of Worth Avenue, at 405 Hibiscus Avenue. Both charge by the hour, but if you purchase an item some shops on Worth Avenue will then validate your ticket, which gives you one hour of free parking.

SHIPPING

Did you perhaps overspend on Worth Avenue and there's no way the content of all those shopping bags is going to fit ino your suitcase?

RSVP will ship anything anywhere. And they will box it up, too. *RSVP. 277 Royal Poinciana Way, 561-659-9077.*

UPS will pack as well as ship. *The UPS Store. 340 Royal Poinciana Way (north side of Royal Poinciana Plaza). 561-655-1071.*

U.S. POST OFFICE

There are two U.S. post offices. One is a block north of Worth Avenue on the corner of South County Road and Peruvian Avenue. The other is on the most northern side of Royal Poinciana Plaza, which is just south of the Royal Poinciana Way.

SUPERMARKETS/PREPARED AND GOURMET FOOD

Amici Market. 155 N. County Rd. 561-832-0201.
C'est Si Bon. 280 Sunset Ave. 561-659-6503.
Publix Supermarket. 135 Bradley Pl. 561-655-4120.

WEATHER

Temperatures rarely dip below the mid-70s from May through September, but they also rarely rise above the low 90s. July and August are the hottest months, but breezes off the ocean are refreshing. In the winter, the temperature rarely falls below the high 50s, and is usually in the 70s during the day. However, there can be isolated winter days when the temperature drops close to freezing and Palm Beachers run around looking for their sweaters. The coldest months are December, January, and February.

INDEX

ABOUT THE AUTHOR

After two decades in publishing in New York City, Pamela Acheson Myers quit the executive suite and escaped to Florida and the Caribbean and wrote about both for *Travel & Leisure*, *Caribbean Travel & Life*, *Florida Travel & Life*, *Berlitz Florida*, and many editions of *Fodor's Caribbean*, *Fodor's Virgin Islands*, and *Fodor's Florida* as well as other Fodor's Guides.

She is the co-author, with her late husband Richard B. Myers, of *The Best of the British Virgin Islands*; *The Best of St. Thomas and St. John, U.S. Virgin Islands*; *The Best Romantic Escapes in Florida, Volume One*; and *The Best Romantic Escapes in Florida, Volume Two*.

Her last book, which she also co-authored with her late husband, is *A Year in Palm Beach: Life in an Alternate Universe*.

Pamela Acheson Myers visited Palm Beach regularly for many years and moved to Palm Beach in 2010. She is an artist as well as an author. Her website is www.circlesintime.com.